Welcome, Reader!

Each day you are becoming a better reader.

In this book, you will see where animals live and how they grow. You will visit the ocean, the desert, and the rain forest. You will even read about tree frogs!

As you read you will learn many new words.

Now turn the page and enjoy the Surprises **inside!**

Houghton Mifflin Reading

Surprises

Senior Authors
J. David Cooper
John J. Pikulski

Authors
David J. Chard
Gilbert Garcia
Claude Goldenberg
Phyllis Hunter
Marjorie Y. Lipson
Shane Templeton
Sheila Valencia
MaryEllen Vogt

Consultants
Linda H. Butler
Linnea C. Ehri
Carla Ford

 HOUGHTON MIFFLIN   BOSTON

Cover illustration by B. Jude Reardon.

Acknowledgments begin on page 232.

Printed in the U.S.A.

ISBN-13: 978-0-618-84812-6
ISBN-10: 0-618-84812-6

1 2 3 4 5 6 7 8 9 10 DOW 12 11 10 09 08 07 06

Surprises

Home Sweet Home

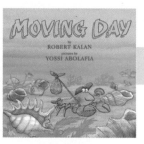

Student Writing Model

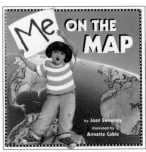

Home Sweet Home

Realistic Fiction

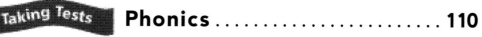

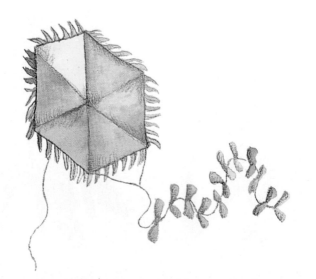

Focus on Genre POETRY

Animal Adventures

Animal Adventures

10

Read Together

Home Sweet Home

The Very Nicest Place

The fish lives in the brook,
The bird lives in the tree,
But home's the very nicest place
For a little child like me.

Anonymous

Background and Vocabulary

Moving Day

MOVING DAY

by
ROBERT KALAN

pictures by
YOSSI ABOLAFIA

Genre **Fantasy**

A Home in a Shell

The next story you will read is about a crab who has grown too big for its shell. Will the crab find a new home?

Words to Know

grow	room
light	these
long	this
more	that's
other	smooth
right	why
small	

Practice Sentences

1. There is no more room to grow in this shell.

2. That's why I must find a new shell.

3. This one is too long.

4. This one is too light.

5. This one is too smooth.

6. These other small shells are not right!

7. This shell is the best match.

MOVING DAY

by
ROBERT KALAN

pictures by
YOSSI ABOLAFIA

Strategy Focus

 As you read the story, ask yourself about the kinds of shells the hermit crab finds.

This shell is snug.

This shell is tight.

I will find a shell that's right.

This shell is too big.

This shell is too small.

Too big, too small,
these shells will not do at all.

21

This shell is too long.

This shell is too wide.

Too long, too wide,
too big, too small,
these shells will not do at all.

This shell is too heavy.

This shell is too light.

28

Too heavy, too light,
too long, too wide,
too big, too small,
these shells will not do at all.

This shell is too rough.

This shell is too smooth.

Too rough, too smooth,
too heavy, too light,
too long, too wide,
too big, too small,
these shells will not do at all.

This shell is too fancy.

This shell is too plain.

Too fancy,

 too plain,

too rough,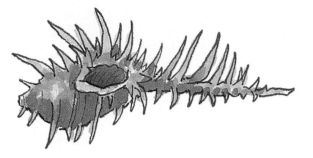

 too smooth,

too heavy,

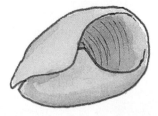 too light,

too long,

 too wide,

too big,

too small,

these shells will
not do at all.

This shell is too —

Wait!

It's NOT too snug.
It's NOT too tight.
This shell is the one that's right.

This shell has more room inside.
Room to grow, room to hide.

I know why this shell is fine.
It's like that other shell of mine.

Meet the Author and the Illustrator

Robert Kalan knows a lot about reading. He was once a kindergarten teacher. Today he likes writing animal stories.

Yossi Abolafia drew cartoons for TV. Now he draws comic strips for newspapers. He tries to tell stories with his pictures.

Internet

To find out more about Robert Kalan and Yossi Abolafia, visit Education Place.

www.eduplace.com/kids

Read Together

Think About the Story

1. Why did it take a long time for the hermit crab to find the right home?

2. What did the crab learn about shells?

3. When will the crab need to find a new home?

Internet

Go on a Web Field Trip

Learn more about crabs and other animals that live at the seashore. Visit Education Place.

www.eduplace.com/kids

Compare Pictures

Look carefully at the color, shape, and size of each shell in the story. Describe to a partner what each shell looks like.

Informing

Write the Answer to a Question

What did the hermit crab learn by the end of the story? Write a sentence to answer the question.

Tips

- Start your sentence with a capital letter.
- End your sentence with a period.

45

Genre

Science Article

Skill: How to Read a Science Article

- **Read** the title.

- **Look** at the photos.

- **Predict** what you will learn.

- **Ask** questions.

- **Reread** if something is not clear.

Hermit Crabs

What's it like to pull your house on your back? Ask a hermit crab — it would know!

Many crabs have a hard shell, but not the hermit crab. Its back is soft.

The hermit must look for a shell that does not have an animal in it. The hermit gets in the shell and pulls it along.

If an animal comes, the crab ducks in the shell and hides.

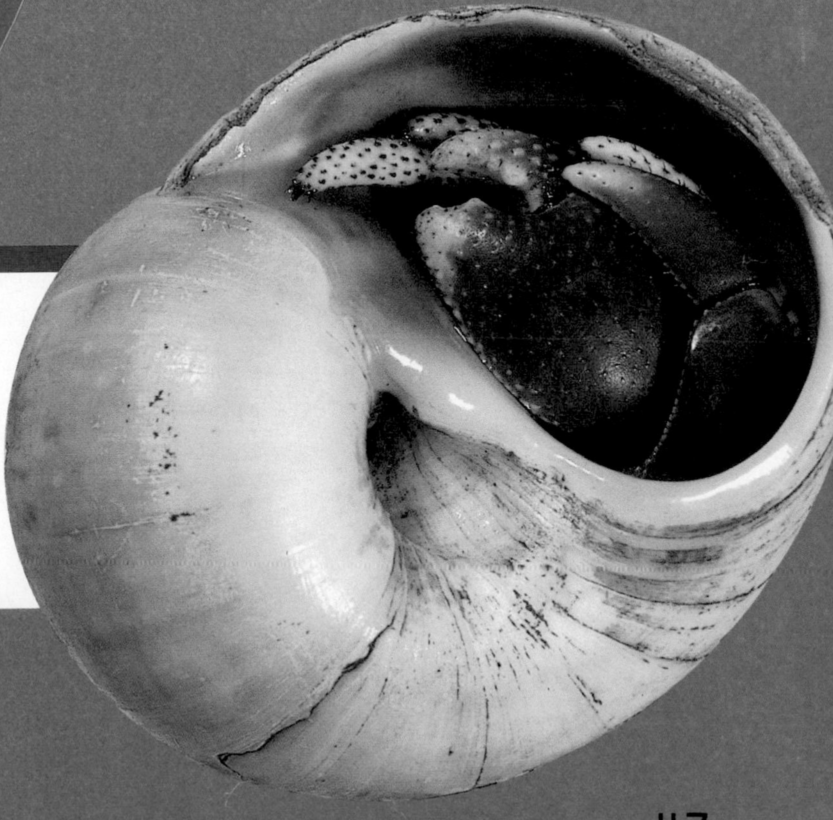

47

If you go to the seashore, look for a shell that walks. Is a hermit in it? What a crab!

Read Together

A Personal Narrative

A personal narrative is a true story about something that happened to the writer. Use this student's writing as a model when you write a personal narrative of your own.

> A good **beginning** tells what the narrative is about.

> **Details** help the reader picture what happened.

The Lost Turtle

I lost my turtle. His name is Herman. I put up signs all around Jacksonville. So every day I sat by the phone. It was not fun when he was gone.

50

I cried and cried. And then when I was walking I saw Herman. We had a party. I was glad he was back.

A good **ending** wraps up the narrative.

Herman

Meet the Author

Hanna N.

Grade: one

State: Florida

Hobbies: drawing and reading

What she'd like to be when she grows up: a daycare teacher

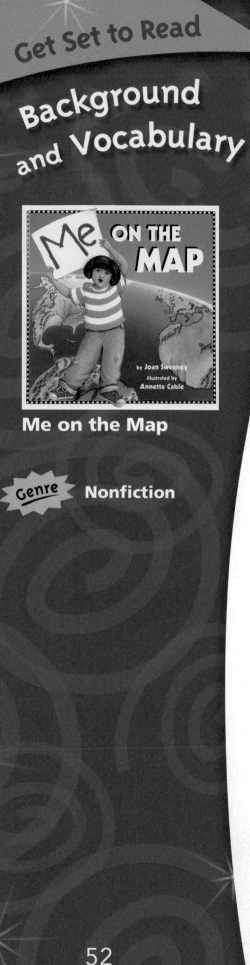

Me on the Map

Genre Nonfiction

Where in the World?

In the next story, you will read about a girl who finds her place on the map. Watch for all the maps she draws!

Words to Know

could	think
house	world
how	state
over	place
own	find
so	

Practice Sentences

1. The world is a big place.

2. Do you think you could find your place on a map?

3. Here's how I do it.

4. I start with my own house and my street.

5. Then I find my town, my state, and my country.

6. So look over a map and find your place on it.

⭐ The United States

Meet the Author and the Illustrator

When she was little, **Joan Sweeney** liked art classes. Later she worked at a newspaper. This is her first book.

Annette Cable's pictures show us what our world looks like. She uses maps to show different places. Her drawings make learning about maps fun.

Internet

You can find out more about Joan Sweeney and Annette Cable at Education Place.

www.eduplace.com/kids

54

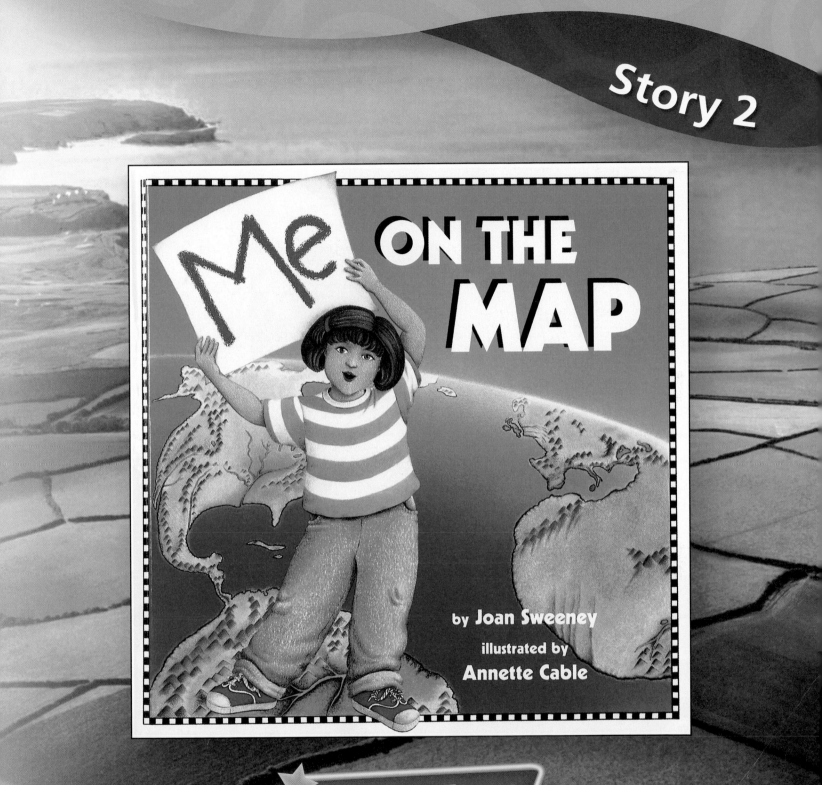

Me ON THE MAP

by Joan Sweeney

illustrated by Annette Cable

Strategy Focus

Read Together — Stop partway through the story and think about some of the places you have seen.

This is me.
This is me in my room.

This is a map of my room.

This is me on the map of my room.

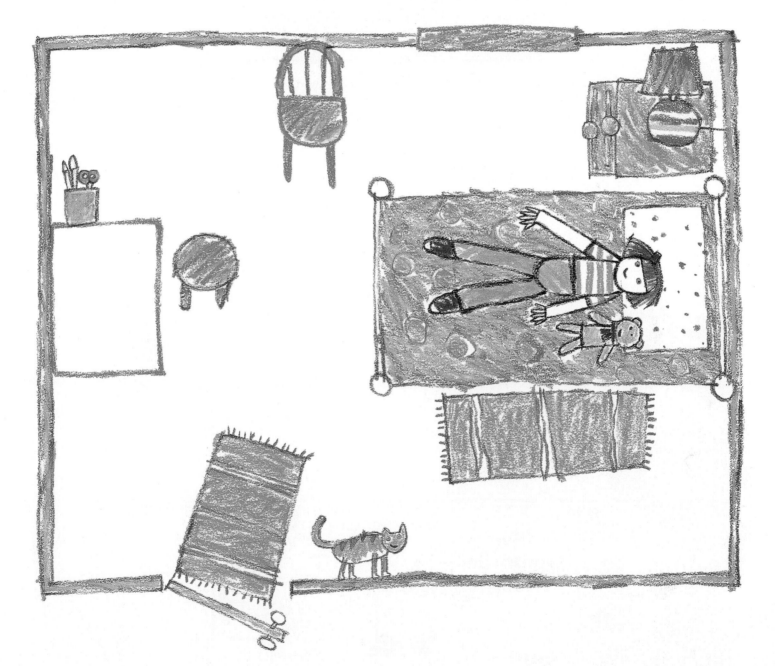

This is my house.

This is a map of my house.

This is my room on the map of my house.

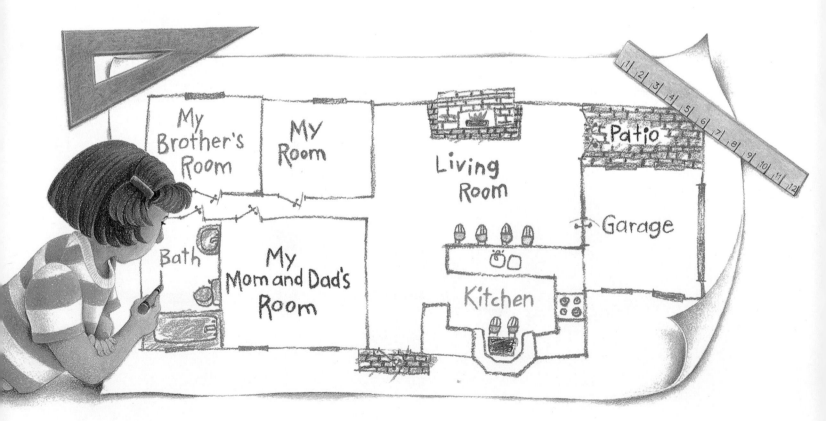

This is my street.

This is a map of my street.

This is my house on the map of my street.

This hermit is much too big for its shell. It must switch shells. Here's a big shell! The hermit pulls out of its first house. Then it pops right in the new one.

48

This is my town.

This is a map of my town.

This is my street on the map of my town.

This is my state.

This is a map of my state.

This is my town on the map of my state.

This is my country.
The United States of America.

This is a map of my country.
This is my state on the map of my country.

This is my world. It is called Earth.
It looks like a giant ball.

If you could unroll the world and make it flat . . .

. . . it would look something like this map of the world.

This is my country on the map of the world.

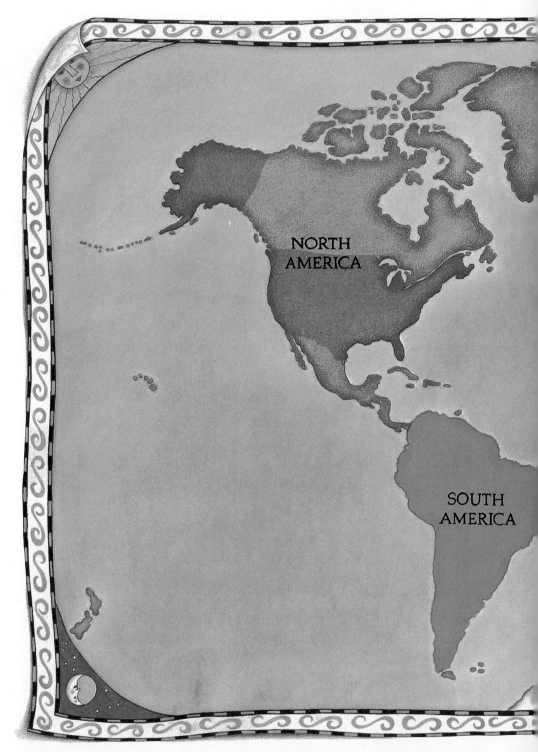

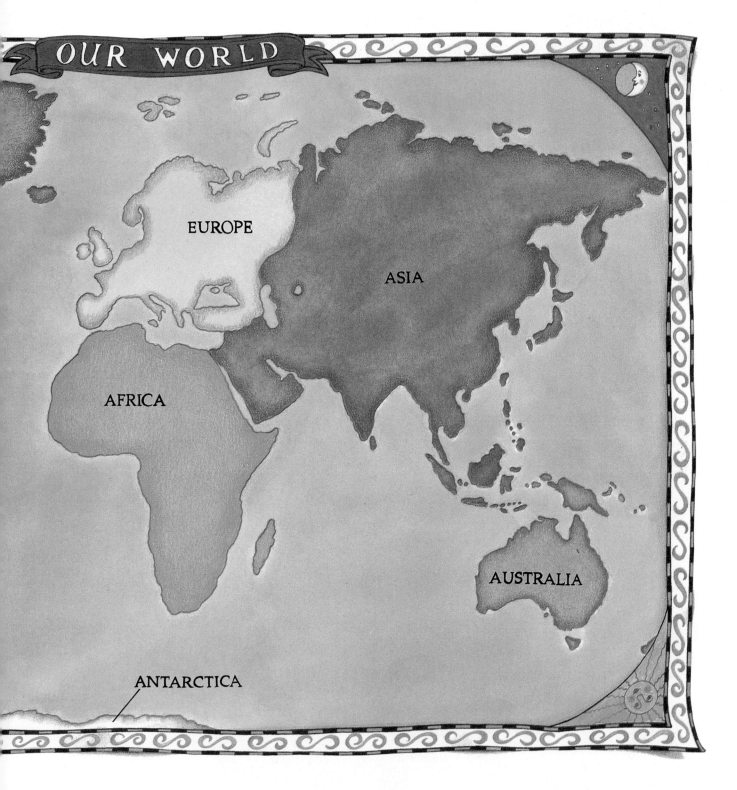

OUR WORLD

EUROPE

ASIA

AFRICA

AUSTRALIA

ANTARCTICA

So here's how I find my special place on the map. First I look at the map of the world and find my country.

OUR WORLD

NORTH AMERICA

SOUTH AMERICA

EUROPE

ASIA

ANT

AUSTRALIA

Then I look at the map of my country
and find my state.
Then I look at the map of my state
and find my town.

Then I look at the map of my town and find my street.

And on my street I find my house.

And in my house I find my room.

And in my room I find me!
Just think . . .

75

. . . in rooms, in houses, on streets, in towns, in countries all over the world, everybody has their own special place on the map.

Just like me.

Just like me on the map.

Read Together

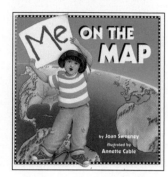
Me ON THE MAP
by Joan Sweeney
Illustrated by Annette Cable

Think About the Story

1. How did the girl learn about her place in the world?

2. How do you think the girl feels about her special place on the map?

3. How would your map be different from the girl's map?

Internet

Complete a Web Word Find

Try finding some of the words from the story in a puzzle. Print out the puzzle from Education Place.

www.eduplace.com/kids

Make a Map

Draw a map of your neighborhood. Include streets, houses, and other buildings you see. Label each place on your map.

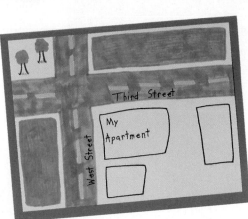

 **Expressing**

Write a Postcard

Write a postcard to a friend. Tell your friend about your special place on the map.

Dear Sam,
My special place is in Los Angeles.

Darren

Los Angeles California

Read
Together

Children of the World

Maps

Skill: How to Read a Map

- This map shows the world.

- It shows land and water.

- The labels tell the names of the continents, countries, and states.

Alaska, USA

NORTH AMERICA

United States of America

New Mexico, USA

USA

USA

SOUTH AMERICA

Children all over the world live in
many different kinds of homes.
Take a look and see where they live!

ASIA

EUROPE

CHINA

China

IVORY COAST

AFRICA

Ivory Coast

AUSTRALIA

ANTARCTICA

83

This girl lives in Alaska.

Her house is made of wood.

This boy lives in New Mexico.

His house is made of adobe.

This boy lives in China.

His house has a grass roof.

This girl lives in the Ivory Coast.

She lives in a tall apartment building.

The Kite

Genre **Realistic Fiction**

Flying a Kite

Next you will read a story about a mother who makes a kite for her children. When the kite gets lost, the children find a surprise.

Words to Know

give	like
good	she'll
her	can't
little	isn't
try	doesn't
was	didn't
fly	it's
our	we've
kite	

Practice Sentences

1. When Mom was little, she had a kite.
2. She didn't know how to fly it.
3. Her father helped her.
4. We have a kite like Mom's.
5. Isn't that nice?
6. She'll try to get our kite up.
7. If we give it a good push, the kite will fly.
8. It's stuck in a tree and can't come down.
9. We've got to make a new kite.
10. Doesn't it look good?

The Kite

Alma Flor Ada

Illustrations by Vivi Escrivá

Strategy Focus

Make sure you understand what is happening in the story as you read.

The good news is . . .
Mama says she'll make us a kite like the ones
her father made when she was little.

The bad news is . . .
Mama doesn't know
how to make a kite.

The good news is . . .
Mama can learn.

The bad news is . . .
A kite isn't easy to make.

The good news is . . .
Mama didn't give up.
What a beautiful kite!

The bad news is . . .
It's raining, so we can't fly our kite.

The good news is . . .
The weather is perfect.
At last, we can fly our kite.

The bad news is . . .
The string broke and
the kite got away.

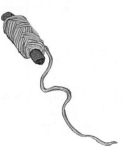

The good news is . . .
Mama says we can try to find it.

The bad news is . . .
We can't find it anywhere.

The good news is . . .
We've found a homeless cat.

The bad news is . . .
Mama says we can't take
the cat home with us.

The good news is . . .
We convinced her.

Meet the Author

Alma Flor Ada learned to read from her grandmother. When she was nine she knew she would be a writer. Now Alma Flor Ada writes books in Spanish and English. She says that the more you read, the better you will write.

Meet the Illustrator

Vivi Escrivá likes drawing pictures of children having fun. When she was little, she won first prize in an art contest. Later Vivi Escrivá worked for a TV show in Spain.

Internet

Learn more about Alma Flor Ada and Vivi Escrivá at Education Place.

www.eduplace.com/kids

Read Together

The Kite
Alma Flor Ada
Illustrations by Vivi Escrivá

Think About the Story

1. How does the mother learn how to make a kite?

2. What do the children learn from their mother?

3. How would it feel if you lost your kite?

Internet

Take an Online Poll

What is your favorite toy? Visit Education Place and take an online poll.

www.eduplace.com/kids

Weather Picture Dictionary

1. Think about the kinds of weather in the story.

2. Draw and label each kind.

3. Add other kinds of weather you know about.

Explaining

Write Sentences

What do you think happened to the kite in the story? Write some sentences to tell about where the kite might be.

Tips

- Make a list of some places the kite could be.
- Make sure each sentence has a naming word and an action word.

Read Together

Genre

Directions

Skill: How to Read Directions

- **Read** the list of materials.

- **Pictures** can give you extra information.

- **Complete** the steps in order.

- **Reread** any part that is unclear.

How to Make a Kite

Materials

- scrap paper

- kite paper (five inches by six inches)

- scissors

- two sticks, five inches and six inches long

- thread

- six feet of ribbon

1 Fold your scrap paper in two. Draw a shape, cut it out, and open it up.

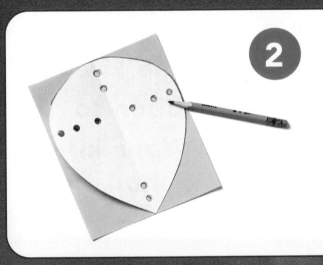

2 Trace your shape onto the kite paper and cut it out. Then make ten holes in your kite.

six-inch stick

3 Lace the two sticks in and out of the holes. Cut ten inches of thread and tie it to the six-inch stick.

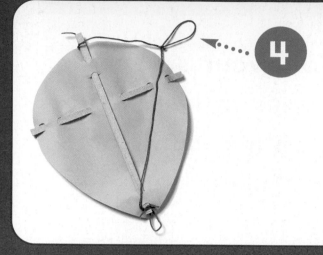

4 Make a loop of thread and tie it to the first thread.

5 Tie a new loop to the bottom of the kite. Tie your ribbon to this loop. Your kite is all set to fly!

Read Together

✓ Phonics

In some tests, your teacher will say a word. You have to find the same sound in another word. Then you fill in the circle to show the correct answer.

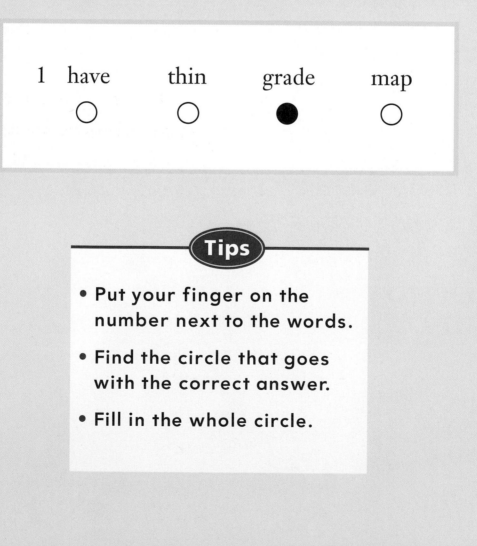

1   have   thin   grade   map
    ○   ○   ●   ○

Tips

- Put your finger on the number next to the words.

- Find the circle that goes with the correct answer.

- Fill in the whole circle.

Now see how one student figured out the right answer.

My teacher said to listen for the vowel sound. Then she said the word **make**.

I say each word to myself to see which one has the same vowel sound as **make**.

I know that **have**, **thin**, and **map** do not have the same vowel sound as **make**. **Grade** has the same sound. I will fill in the circle under **grade**.

Focus on Genre

Poetry

Poetry uses words in interesting ways. Some poems have words that **rhyme**. Some poems are made of parts, or **stanzas**. Some poems **describe** things or tell **stories**. Look and listen to what these poems do.

CONTENTS

Turtle, turtle

Turtle, turtle,
I wonder why
Other animals
Pass you by?

Turtles travel
Very slow,
Still I get
Where I want to go.

by Langston Hughes

114

Quack, Quack!

We have two ducks. One blue. One black.
And when our blue duck goes "Quack-quack"
our black duck quickly quack-quacks back.
The quacks Blue quacks make her quite a quacker
but Black is a quicker quacker-backer.

by Dr. Seuss

Morning Sun

warming up
my bed
in the morning

the Sun
calls me
through the window

"wake up
get up
come on out"

by Francisco X. Alarcón

Sol matutino

calentando
mi cama
en la mañana

el Sol
me llama
por la ventana

"despierta
levántate
ven afuera"

por Francisco X. Alarcón

The Chipmunk

Chitter-chatter, chitter-chatter
is the chipmunk's steady patter,
even when he's eating acorns
(which he hopes will make him fatter).

by Jack Prelutsky

A little egg
in a nest of hay.
cheep-cheep.
crack-crack.
a little chick
pecked his shell away
cheep-cheep.
crack-crack.

by Tina Anthony
Age 7
England

A discovery!
On my frog's smooth green belly
there sits no button.

Haiku, Yayû

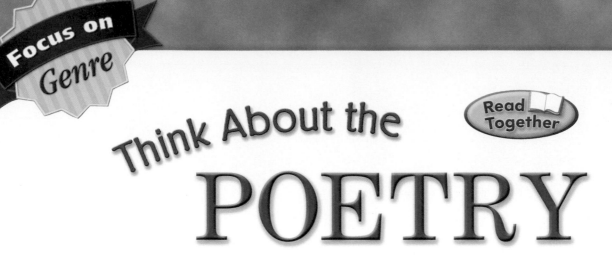

Think About the
POETRY

Read Together

1. How is "A discovery" like "Quack, Quack!"? How is it different?

2. Look back at the poem "Morning Sun." How does the poet feel when the sun wakes him up?

3. Which animal poem do you think describes the animal best? What words describe the animal?

4. Which poem is your favorite? Why?

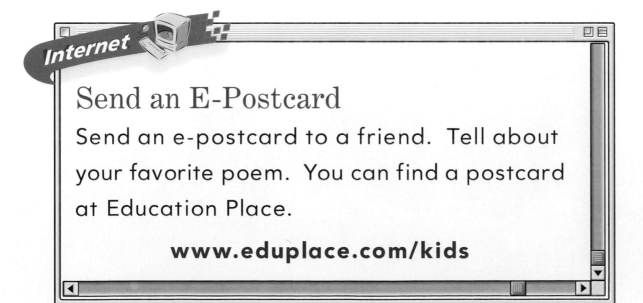

Internet

Send an E-Postcard
Send an e-postcard to a friend. Tell about your favorite poem. You can find a postcard at Education Place.

www.eduplace.com/kids

Creating

Write a Poem

You can write your own poem. Here's how to do it:

1. Choose a subject that you want to write about.
2. Decide if your poem will have rhyming words.
3. Think of some interesting ways to describe your subject.

When you finish, share your poem with others. Make a class poetry book by putting all your poems together.

Animal Adventures

Two Feet, Four Feet

I have only two small feet,
But horses, dogs, and cows
   Have four.
I can walk and run with
   Mine.
So why do **they** need any
   More?

by Ilo Orleans

The Sleeping Pig

written by Carmen Tafolla and Jan Epton Seale
illustrated by Rosario Valderrama

The Sleeping Pig

Genre **Fantasy**

How to Wake a Pig

In the next story, you'll read about a pig who won't get out of a watermelon patch. A small hero finally gets the pig to move.

Words to Know

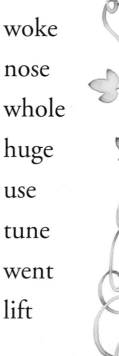

morning	woke
found	nose
shout	whole
by	huge
out	use
show	tune
climb	went
go	lift
home	

Practice Sentences

1. If you went by your bed one morning and found a huge pig, would you lift it out?

2. You could walk by and shout, "Go home!"

3. Then climb up and tap the pig's small nose.

4. Sing a tune.

5. You could use the whole day to wake the pig.

6. Once you woke the pig, you could show it how to get home.

Good Morning

Meet the Authors

Carmen Tafolla

Jan Epton Seale

The authors first wrote this story in Spanish. Carmen Tafolla and Jan Epton Seale both live in Texas. Jan Epton Seale lives near Mexico. Carmen Tafolla has a daughter named Mari.

Internet

You can learn more about Carmen Tafolla and Jan Epton Seale at Education Place.

www.eduplace.com/kids

The Sleeping Pig

written by Carmen Tafolla and Jan Epton Seale

illustrated by Rosario Valderrama

Strategy Focus

Read Together As you read, stop and think about what each animal does to wake Mrs. Pig.

133

One morning, Celina found a huge pig sleeping in the watermelon patch.

Celina began to shout. "Go home, Mrs. Pig! I wish you would go. You can't rest here in the watermelon patch. I can't pick my watermelons."

But huge Mrs. Pig didn't wake up.

138

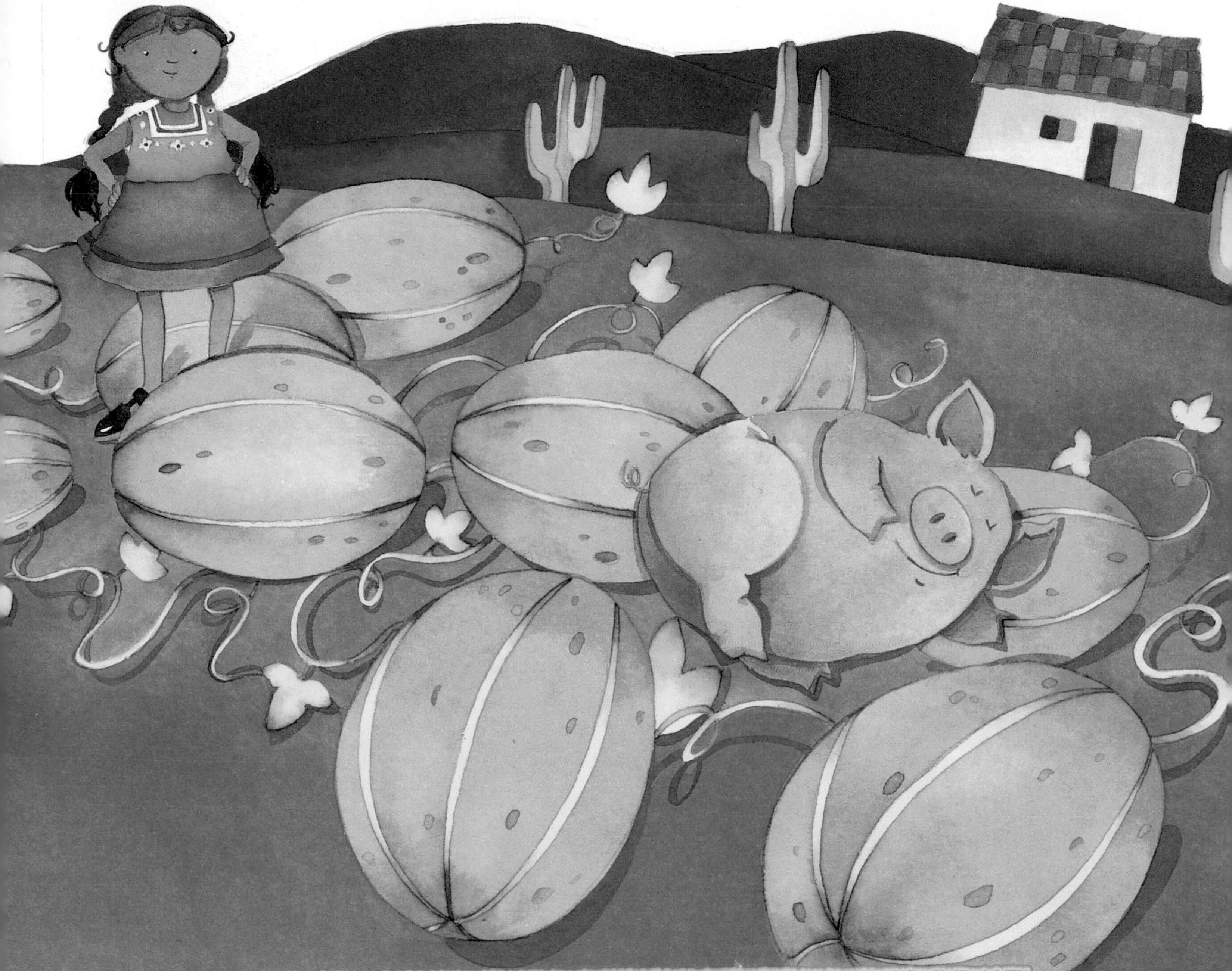

A coyote came by and said, "Let me show you how to get Mrs. Pig out of the patch." The coyote began to howl and howl.

But huge Mrs. Pig did not wake up.

139

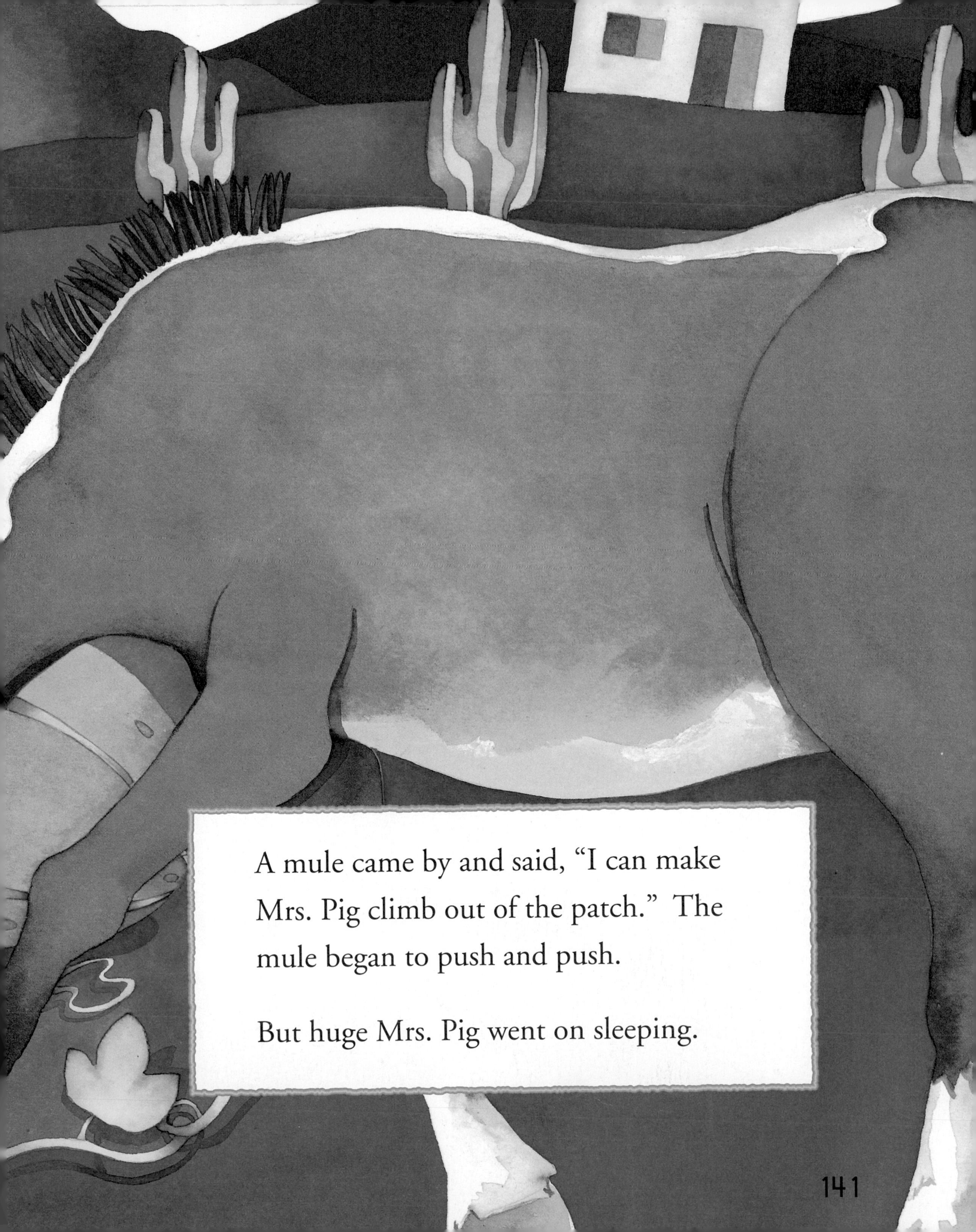

A mule came by and said, "I can make Mrs. Pig climb out of the patch." The mule began to push and push.

But huge Mrs. Pig went on sleeping.

A rabbit came by and said, "I will get Mrs. Pig out of the patch for you." The rabbit began to hop and hop.

But huge Mrs. Pig went on sleeping.

A snake came by and said, "I will use my tail to lift Mrs. Pig out of the patch." The snake began to pull and pull.

But huge Mrs. Pig wouldn't wake up.

Then a cricket came by and said, "I know I am small and Mrs. Pig is huge. But just look at what I can do."

The cricket began to sing a tune.
Chirrr-chirrr-chirrr! Di-di-di-di!

Mrs. Pig woke up fast. "Yes, it's time to go home," she said with her nose up. "A watermelon patch does not make a good bed." And she left, sulking.

Celina thanked the small cricket. Then
they ate a whole watermelon to celebrate!

Meet the Illustrator
Rosario Valderrama

Rosario Valderrama was born in Mexico City. When she draws, she tries to remember the things she loved as a child. She says young artists should try to show their worlds to others.

Internet

To find out more about Rosario Valderrama, visit Education Place. **www.eduplace.com/kids**

Responding

The Sleeping Pig
written by Carmen Tafolla and Jan Epton Seale
illustrated by Rosario Valderrama

Think About the Story

1. How did Celina feel when she saw Mrs. Pig?

2. Why was the cricket the only animal who could wake Mrs. Pig?

3. What would you do if you were Celina?

Print Out Puppets

Print out story character puppets from Education Place to retell the story.

www.eduplace.com/kids

154

Make an Award

Make an award for the hero in the story. Write a title for your award.

Explaining

Write a Poster

How would you wake a sleeping pig? Draw a poster and write one sentence. Share your poster with the class.

Tips

- **Think about some ways to wake up a pig.**
- **Make sure that your drawing and your sentence match.**

Genre

**Social Studies
Article**

**Skill: How to
Read a Social
Studies Article**

- **Look** at the
  title and
  pictures.

- **Think** about
  what you
  know.

- **Predict** what
  you will learn.

- **Reread** if you
  do not
  understand.

What Is a Desert?

A desert is a dry place that gets little or no rain. There are many deserts all over the world.

Cactus plants can grow in a desert. They can hold water for a long time. Some cactuses are as big as trees.

Arizona, USA

Namibia, Africa

Flowering Agave

Saguaro cactus

Claret Cup cactus

157

Birds, mice, snakes, and lizards are some of the animals that live in the desert.

The scorpion also makes its home in the desert.

Ostrich

Flap-Necked Chameleon

Rattlesnake

Scorpion

Some people move through the desert on camels. Camels can go days without food or water.

Would you like to see a desert?

Read
Together

A Description

A description is a picture in words that
helps the reader to see, hear, taste, feel,
and smell what you're writing about.
Use this student writing as a model when
you write your own description.

A good
beginning tells
what the
description is
about.

A good
description
includes **sense**
words.

Fishing with My Dad

I have a big fishing rod with a small
hook at the end. When I go fishing
with my Dad, this is what I use. My
Dad's fishing rod is tall and yellow
with a big hook at the end.

He usually catches huge gray catfish.
I usually catch small minnows.

Meet the Author

Megan S.

Grade: one

State: Delaware

Hobbies: fishing, reading, and writing

What she'd like to be when she grows up: a teacher

EEK! There's a Mouse in the House

Genre **Fantasy**

Animals in the House

In the next story, you'll read about some animals that mess up a little girl's house! How can she get rid of them?

Words to Know

cow	wall
table	me
now	he
door	EEK
there	sheep
through	eating
horse	

Practice Sentences

1. A cow, a sheep, and a horse came to a house.
2. "Now what could be in there?" asked the horse.
3. He went through the door.
4. The others went through, too.
5. By the wall was a table of things to eat.
6. A mouse was eating on the table.
7. "EEK!" said the cow and the sheep.
8. "The mouse can't hurt me," said the horse.

EEK!
There's a Mouse in the House

WONG HERBERT YEE

⭐ **Strategy Focus**

Read Together As you read the story, ask yourself about each animal and what it does.

EEK!

There's a mouse in the house.

Send in the cat
to chase that rat!

Uh-oh!

The cat knocked over a lamp.

Send in the dog
to catch that scamp!

Dear me!

The dog has broken a dish.

And now the cat is after the fish.

Send in the hog
to shoo that dog!

Oh my!

The hog is eating the cake.

Sending the hog
was a big mistake.

Send in the cow.

Send that cow NOW!

Oh no!

The cow is dancing
with a mop.

Send in the sheep
to make her stop!

Goodness!

The sheep is tangled
in yarn.

Send in the hen
from the barn!

Mercy!

The hen is laying eggs
on the table.

Send in the horse
from the stable!

Heavens!

The horse kicked a hole in the wall.

Send in the elephant to get rid of them ALL!

The elephant was BIG,
but he squeezed through the door.

Once he was in,
there was room for no more.

Out of the house marched the cat and the cow.

Out came the horse and the hen and the hog.

Out walked the sheep.

Out ran the dog.

But then from within,
there came a shout:

EEK! There's a mouse in the house!

Meet the Author and Illustrator

This is **Wong Herbert Yee**'s first children's book. While he was writing it, he read it to his young daughter, Ellen. If she laughed at a sentence, he kept it in the story.

Internet

Find out more about Wong Herbert Yee at Education Place.

www.eduplace.com/kids

Read
Together

EEK!
There's a Mouse in the House

WONG HERBERT YEE

Think About the Story

1. How did the girl feel about the mouse?

2. Was it a good idea for the girl to call in the animals? Why?

3. What would you do if you were the girl in this story?

Internet

Take an Online Poll

What animal from *EEK! There's a Mouse in the House* would you want for a pet? Visit Education Place to place your vote.

www.eduplace.com/kids

Act Out the Story

Act out the story with some partners. Each of you can be a different character. Make sure to use each character's actions.

Informing

Write a List

Pick an animal from the story. Make a list of clean-up chores for the animal.

Cat
1. Pick up the lamp.

Tips

- **Think about what the animal needs to clean up.**
- **Number each thing on your list.**

Animals Big and Small

Animals come in many shapes and sizes. Let's look at some of the biggest and smallest animals in the world.

Genre

Pictographs

Skill: How to Read a Pictograph

- A pictograph is a chart that uses pictures to compare things.

- These pictographs show the size of animals compared to people.

- The biggest animal in the world is the blue whale. It can grow to 100 feet long. That's longer than sixteen six-foot men lying head to toe!

Giraffes are the tallest animals in the world. Some giraffes grow as tall as nineteen feet. That's taller than three men standing on top of each other's shoulders!

Harvest Mouse

Some harvest mice are no more than three inches long. That's about as long as a grown-up's finger!

Bee Hummingbird

The bee hummingbird from Cuba is just two inches long. That's shorter than a grown-up's thumb!

Red-Eyed Tree Frog

BY JOY COWLEY · PHOTOGRAPHS BY NIC BISHOP

 Nonfiction

A Visit to the Rain Forest

You will read about a day in the life of a red-eyed tree frog in the next story.

Words to Know

been	evening
far	near
forest	rain
goes	wait
hungry	day
soon	away

Practice Sentences

1. My mom has been to the rain forest.

2. It's far away from where we live.

3. I will go the next time Mom goes.

4. We will hike all day.

5. When we are hungry, we will stop and eat.

6. We will spend the evening in a tent.

7. We will sit near a tree and wait for a red-eyed tree frog.

8. I hope we go soon!

RED-EYED TREE FROG

BY JOY COWLEY · PHOTOGRAPHS BY NIC BISHOP

Strategy Focus

Read Together

What do you think the red-eyed tree frog will do? Read the story to find out.

Evening comes to the rain forest.

The macaw
and the toucan
will soon go to sleep.

But the red-eyed tree frog has
been asleep all day.

It wakes up hungry.
What will it eat?

Here is an iguana.
Frogs do not eat iguanas.

Do iguanas eat frogs?
The red-eyed tree frog does
not wait to find out.
It hops onto another branch.

The frog is hungry but it will
not eat the ant.

It will not eat the katydid.

Will it eat the caterpillar?
No!

The caterpillar is poisonous.

Something moves near the frog.
Something slips and slithers along a branch.
It is a hungry boa snake.

The snake flicks its tongue.
It tastes frog in the air.
Look out, frog!

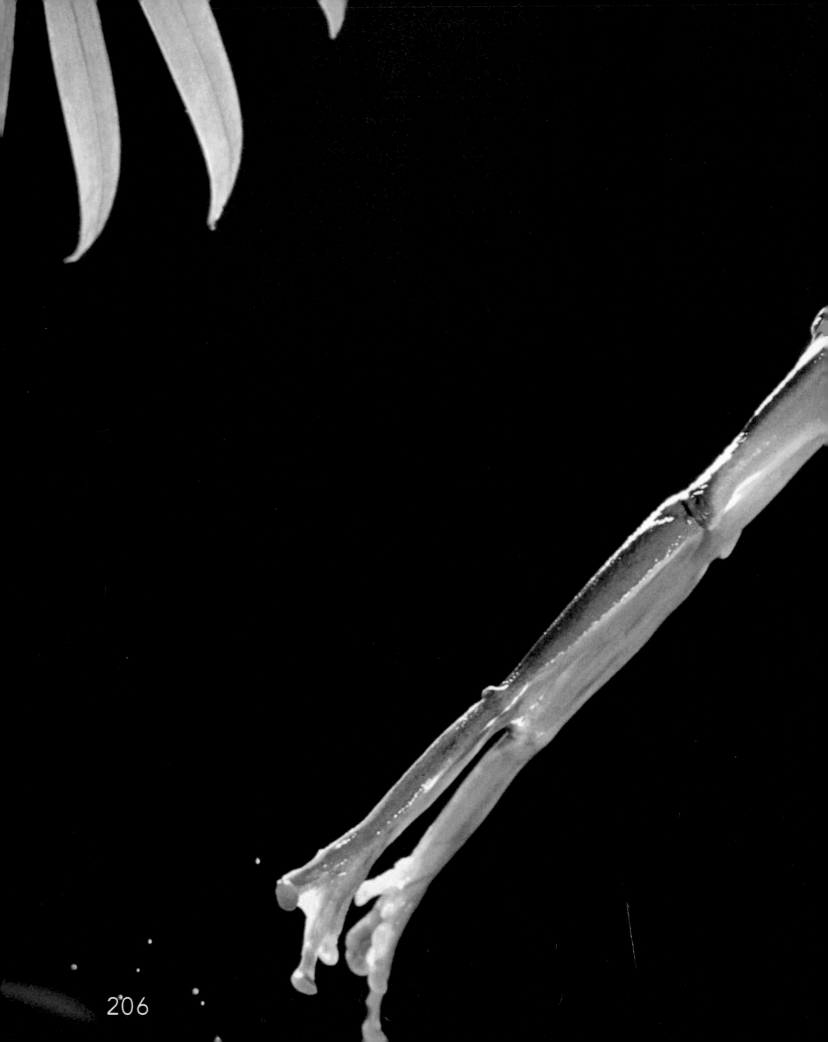

JUMP!

JUMP!

The frog lands on a leaf,
far away from the boa.
What does the frog see on
the leaf?

A moth!

Crunch, crunch, crunch!

The tree frog is no longer hungry.
It climbs onto a leaf.

The red-eyed tree frog shuts its eyes . . .

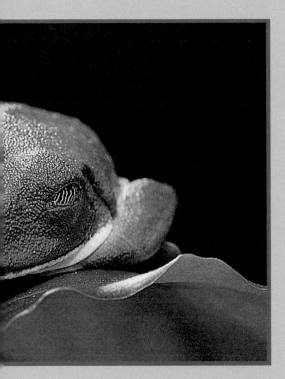

and goes to sleep . . .

as morning comes to the rain forest.

214

Meet the Author and the Photographer

Joy Cowley loves animals, especially frogs. When she saw these pictures, she liked them very much. She decided to write a children's book to go with them.

Nic Bishop went to the rain forest to take photographs of the red-eyed tree frogs. One frog became a family pet.

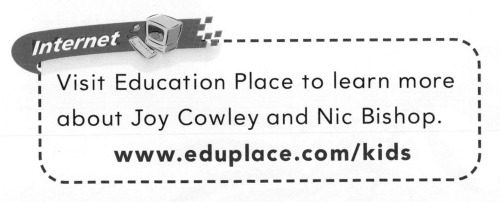

Internet

Visit Education Place to learn more about Joy Cowley and Nic Bishop.

www.eduplace.com/kids

215

Read Together

Think About the Story

1. Do you think this rain forest is quiet or noisy? Why?

2. What do you think the red-eyed tree frog has learned about living in the rain forest?

3. Would you like to visit the rain forest? Why?

Internet

Go on a Web Field Trip

Visit a rain forest at Education Place.

www.eduplace.com/kids

Comparing Sizes

A red-eyed tree frog is nearly as long as this ruler. Find things in your classroom that are about the same size.

Creating

Write a Riddle

Write a riddle about one of the animals in the story. Have a partner read your riddle and guess the animal.

Tips

- Study a picture of the animal.
- Use describing words.

Who has a yellow stripe and many legs?

Poetry Link

Read Together

Genre

Poetry

Skill: How to Read a Poem

- **Read** the title to see what the poem is about.

- **Read** the poem.

- **Listen** for any rhyming words.

The Snake

Don't ever make
the bad mistake
of stepping on
the sleeping snake

because
his jaws

might be awake.

by Jack Prelutsky

Snake, 20th century,
Niki de Saint-Phalle, b. 1930, French
painted polyester

THE TOUCAN

Of all the birds I know, few can
Boast of as large a bill as the toucan.
Yet I can think of one who can,
And if you think a while, too, you can:
Another toucan
In the zoo can.

by Pyke Johnson, Jr.

Toucan Design on Mola, San Blas Archipelago, Panama

Filling in the Blank

Some tests have sentences with a blank in them. You must decide which answer choice best fills in the blank. Look at this sample test for *Red-Eyed Tree Frog*. The correct answer is shown.

Read the sentence. Fill in the circle next to the best answer.

1   The red-eyed tree frog _____ all day.

   ● sleeps   ○ climbs   ○ eats

Tips

- Put your finger on the number next to the sentence.

- Find the circle that goes with the correct answer.

- Fill in the whole circle.

220

Now see how one student figured out the best answer.

First, I read the directions. Then I read the test sentence. I need to find out what the frog does all day.

I look back in the story. The beginning tells what the frog does. I will look there.

I read the test sentence to myself, using each answer choice. The last two choices do not tell about the frog in the daytime. The first choice is best.

Visit **www.eduplace.com** for
e • **Glossary** and *e* • **Word Game.**

A

anywhere

Anywhere means in any place. You can sit **anywhere** you like.

B

ball

A **ball** is something that is round. Miguel hit the **ball** with the bat.

barn

A **barn** is a kind of building on a farm. A farmer keeps his cows and pigs in the **barn**.

beautiful

Beautiful means very nice to look at or hear. Anna drew a picture of a **beautiful** rainbow.

began

To **begin** means to start. School **began** in September.

boa

A **boa** is a kind of snake. A **boa** can live in the rain forest.

C

caterpillar

A **caterpillar** is an insect that looks like a worm. A **caterpillar** will change into a butterfly.

celebrate

To **celebrate** is to do something special for an event. We went to the park to **celebrate** my birthday.

convinced

To **convince** means to talk someone into something. I **convinced** my mother to let me go on the trip.

country

A **country** is a place where people live and share the same laws. There are many **countries** in the world.

coyote

A **coyote** is an animal that looks like a small wolf. The **coyote** didn't look much bigger than a dog.

cricket

A **cricket** is a small insect that looks like a grasshopper. Jamal saw the **cricket** jump.

D

dancing

To **dance** means to move your body to music. Jan and her friends like **dancing** at parties.

E

Earth

Earth is the planet we live on. **Earth** looks round when you see it from space.

easy

Easy means not hard to do. Riding my bike is **easy**.

elephant

An **elephant** is a very big animal with thick skin, big ears, and a long trunk. The **elephant** was the biggest animal in the circus.

eyes

Eyes are the parts of the body that let it see. The kitten closed its **eyes** and went to sleep.

F

fancy

Fancy means prettier or better than usual. We had a **fancy** cake at the party.

G

giant

Giant means much bigger than usual. Michael looked up at the **giant** tree.

H

heavy
Heavy means hard to lift. The box of toys was too **heavy** to carry.

hide
To **hide** something is to put it where nobody will see it. When I **hide**, my friends can't find me.

howl
To **howl** is to make a long cry like a dog, coyote, or wolf. My dog will **howl** when she's lonely.

I

iguana
An **iguana** is a kind of lizard. Tanya wanted an **iguana** for a pet.

inside
To be **inside** means to be in something. I'm staying **inside** the house because it's raining.

K

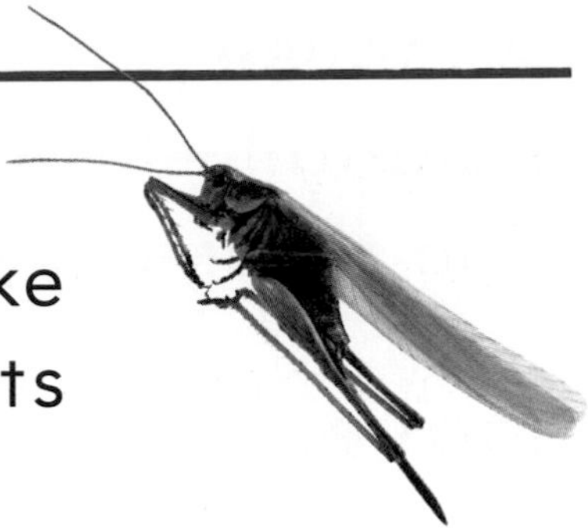

katydid

A **katydid** is a large green insect like a grasshopper. A **katydid** will rub its wings together to make a noise.

L

laying

To **lay** an egg is to make an egg. The hen was **laying** eggs in her nest.

M

macaw

A **macaw** is a large parrot.
The **macaw** has a strong, curved beak.

marched

To **march** with someone is to take the same size steps at the same time. The band **marched** in the big parade.

mercy

To say **Mercy** is to show surprise. **Mercy!** That was a close call.

mouse

A **mouse** is a very small animal with a
long tail, short fur, and sharp teeth.
The **mouse** likes to eat cheese.

moves

To **move** is to go from one place to another.
A bird **moves** from tree to tree by flying.

N

news

News is a story about things that are
happening. My mother watches the **news**
on television.

P

perfect

If something is **perfect**, it is just right.
It was a **perfect** day for flying our kite.

plain

Plain means very simple. I put my lunch
in a **plain** brown paper bag.

poisonous

A **poison** is something that can cause sickness or death. A rattlesnake is a **poisonous** animal.

R

rabbit

A **rabbit** is an animal with long ears and soft fur. A **rabbit** can hop very fast.

raining

To **rain** means to fall as drops of water. Get your umbrella because it's **raining**.

rough

Something that is **rough** does not feel even. The bumpy road was very **rough**.

S

smooth

Something that is **smooth** feels even and has no rough spots. The ice at the rink was very **smooth**.

special

Special means important and not like all the rest. Holidays and birthdays are **special** days.

street

A **street** is a road in a city or town. Sue lives on a busy **street**.

T

tail

A **tail** is part of an animal's body. Laura's dog wags its **tail** when it gets a treat.

tangled

Tangle means to be all mixed up. The kite's string got **tangled** in the tree.

tongue

The **tongue** is a part of the body inside the mouth. Your **tongue** helps you eat and speak.

toucan

A **toucan** is a colorful bird with a very long, large bill. Amy was excited to see a **toucan** flying in the rain forest.

town

A **town** is a place where people live and work. My **town** is smaller than a city.

W

wait

To **wait** means to stay someplace until something happens. We **wait** at the corner until the school bus comes.

watermelon

A **watermelon** is a big sweet fruit that is pink or red inside. **Watermelon** is a good snack in the summer.

weather

Weather is what it is like outside. Jim goes swimming in warm **weather**.

Acknowledgments

For each of the selections listed below, grateful acknowledgment is made for permission to excerpt and/or reprint original or copyrighted material, as follows:

Selections

EEK! There's a Mouse in the House, by Wong Herbert Yee. Copyright © 1992 by Wong Herbert Yee. Reprinted by permission of Houghton Mifflin Company. All rights reserved.

The Kite, by Alma Flor Ada, illustrated by Vivi Escrivá. Copyright © 1999 by Santillana USA Publishing Co., Inc. Reprinted by permission of the publisher.

Me on the Map, by Joan Sweeney, illustrated by Annette Cable. Text copyright © 1996 by Joan Sweeney. Illustrations copyright © 1996 by Annette Cable. Published by arrangement with Random House Children's Books, a division of Random House, Inc., New York, New York, U.S.A. All rights reserved.

Moving Day, by Robert Kalan, illustrated by Yossi Abolafia. Text copyright © 1996 by Robert Kalan. Illustrations copyright © 1996 by Yossi Abolafia. Reprinted by permission of HarperCollins Publishers.

Red-Eyed Tree Frog, by Joy Cowley, photographs by Nic Bishop, published by Scholastic Press, a division of Scholastic Inc. Text copyright © 1999 by Joy Cowley, Photographs copyright © 1999 by Nic Bishop. Reprinted by permission of Scholastic Inc.

Poetry

"A discovery!" by Yayû, translated by Sylvia Cassedy and Kunihiro Suetake, from *Birds, Frogs and Moonlight.* Copyright © 1967 by Doubleday and Co. Reprinted by permission of Ellen Cassedy.

"A little egg," by Tina Anthony from *Miracles: Poems by Children of the English Speaking World,* edited by Richard Lewis. Copyright © 1966 by Richard Lewis. Used with permission of Richard Lewis.

"The Chipmunk" from *Zoo Doings,* by Jack Prelutsky. Copyright © 1983 by Jack Prelutsky. Reprinted by permission of HarperCollins Publishers.

"Morning Sun/Sol matutino" from *Laughing Tomatoes and Other Spring Poems/Jitomates risueños y otros poemas de primavera,* by Francisco X. Alarcón. Copyright © 1997 by Francisco Alarcón. Reprinted by permission of the publisher, Children's Book Press, San Francisco, CA.

"Quack, Quack!" from *Oh Say Can You Say?,* by Dr. Seuss, TM & Copyright © by Dr. Seuss Enterprises, L.P., 1979. Reprinted by permission of Random House Children's Books, a division of Random House, Inc.

"The Snake" from *Zoo Doings,* by Jack Prelutsky. Copyright © 1983 by Jack Prelutsky. Reprinted by permission of HarperCollins Publishers.

"The Toucan" from *Pyke's Poems,* by Pyke Johnson, Jr., published by Shorelands Publishing Company. Copyright © by Pyke Johnson, Jr. Reprinted by permission of the author.

"Turtle, turtle" from *The Sweet and Sour Animal Book,* by Langston Hughes. Copyright © 1994 (text) by Romana Bass & Arnold Rampersad, Administrators of the Estate of Langston Hughes. Used by permission of Oxford University Press, Inc., and Harold Ober Associates, Inc.

"Two Feet, Four Feet," by Ilo Orleans. Copyright © 1992 by Ilo Orleans. Reprinted by permission of Karen S. Solomon.

Illustration from *Waiting for Wings,* by Lois Ehlert, is depicted on the Focus on Poetry Table of Contents page. Copyright © 2001 by Lois Ehlert. Reprinted by permission of Harcourt, Inc.

Special thanks to the following teachers whose students' compositions appear as Student Writing Models: Cheryl Claxton, Florida; Patricia Kopay, Delaware; Susana Llanes, Michigan; Joan Rubens, Delaware; Nancy Schulten, Kentucky; Linda Wallis, California

Credits

Photography

3 (t) Navaswan/Taxi/Getty Images. (b) Siede Preis/PhotoDisc Green/Getty Images. **5,6** © Navaswan/Taxi/Getty Images. **7** (l) © PhotoDisc/Getty Images. (r) Tim Davis/Photo Researchers, Inc. **9,11** © Siede Preis/PhotoDisc Green/Getty Images. **12-13** (bkgd) From *Look-Alikes, Jr.* by Joan Steiner. Copyright © 1999 by Joan Steiner. Photography by Thomas Lindley. **13** (m) © Navaswan/Taxi/Getty Images. **16** (bkgd) © Georgette Douwma/Taxi/Getty Images. **43** (t) Courtesy William Morrow. **44** (l) © PhotoDisc/Getty Images. (r) Artville. **46** (t) CORBIS/Stuart Westmorland. (b) J.H. (Pete) Carmichael. **47** (t) Dave King/Dorling Kindersley. (b) J.H. (Pete) Carmichael. **48** NHPA/Anthony Bannister. **49** CORBIS/Annie Griffiths Belt. **54** (t) John Zich/Mercury Pictures. (b) Courtesy Annette Cable. **54-5** (bkgd) © Charles O'Rear/Corbis. **82** (t) Chris Arend/Alaska Stock Images. (b) Rubberball Productions. **83** (t) Jian Chen/Stock Connection/PictureQuest. (b) Michael Dwyer/Stock Boston/PictureQuest. **84** (tl) Chris Arend/Alaska Stock Images. (tr) CORBIS/Galen Rowell. (bl) Garry Adams/ IndexStock. (br) Rubberball Productions. **85** (tl) CORBIS/The Purcell Team. (tr) Jian Chen/Stock Connection/PictureQuest. (bl) Michael Dwyer/Stock Boston/PictureQuest. (br) Christopher Morris/Black Star/PictureQuest. **88-9** (bkgd) © Zephyr Picture/ Index Stock Imagery/PictureQuest. **102** Courtesy Alma Flor Ada. **103** Courtesy Vivi Escrivá. **106–9** (bkgd) © PhotoDisc/Getty Images. **108** Lynda Richardson. **109** (t) Lawrence Migdale/Stock Boston. (b) Lynda Richardson. **114–5** © PhotoDisc/Getty Images. **116** Tim Davis/Stone/Getty Images. **117** Paul Chauncey/CORBIS. **118** Laurie Rubin/The Image Bank/Getty Images. **120** Daniel J. Cox/Stone/Getty Images. **122–3** Tim Davis/Photo Researchers, Inc. **124–5** Frank Moscati/CORBIS. **126** John Lei/Stock Boston. **128-9** (bkgd) © Ariel Skelley/CORBIS. **129** (m) © Siede Preis/PhotoDisc Green/Getty Images. **132** (l) Courtesy Carmen Tafolla. (r) Paul Buck/Mercury Pictures. **132-3** (bkgd) Kathryn Kleinman/FoodPix/Getty Images. **153** Courtesy Rosario Valeramma. **156–7** © Jim Brandenburg/Minden Pictures. **156** (bl) © Carr Clifton/Minden Pictures. (br) © Jim Brandenburg/Minden Pictures. **157** (bl) Frans Lanting/Minden Pictures. (bm) Brian Stablyk/Stone/Getty Images. (br) Kerrick James/Stone/Getty Images. **158** (t) (m) (bl) Frans Lanting/Minden Pictures. (br) © Jim Brandenburg/Minden Pictures. **159** Will & Deni McIntyre/Stone/ Getty Images. **160** © PhotoDisc/Getty Images. **164-5** (bkgd) © Albert Normandin/Masterfile. **183** Courtesy Wong Herbert Yee. **186–7** Mike Johnson Marine Natural History Photography. **188** Corbis Royalty Free. **189** (t) CORBIS/ George McCarthy. (b) Robert Tyrrell Photography. **190** © Nic Bishop Photography. **192** (bkgd) © R. Watts/Premium/ Panoramic Images. **215** (tl) © Terry Coles. (tr) Michael P.L. Fogden/ Bruce Coleman/PictureQuest. (bl) David Aubrey/CORBIS. (br) Courtesy Nic Bishop. **216** © PhotoDisc/Getty Images. **217** CORBIS/David A. Northcott. **218** Snake, 20th century. Niki de Saint-Phalle, b. 1930, French. painted polyester. 59 in height. Private Collection. Christie's Images, Inc. **219** CORBIS/Kevin Schafer. **222** © PhotoDisc/Getty Images. **223** Kim Taylor/Dorling Kindersley. **224** © PhotoDisc/Getty Images. **225** © PhotoDisc/Getty Images. **226** PhotoSpin. **227** (t) Artville. (b) © PhotoDisc/Getty Images. **228** © PhotoDisc/Getty Images. **229** © PhotoDisc/Getty Images. **231** (t) ©Frans Lanting/Minden Pictures. (b) Artville.

Assignment Photography

15, 45 (t), **53, 80. 105** © HMCo./Joel Benjamin. **111, 221** © HMCo./Michael Indresano Photography. **131, 163, 184** © HMCo./Michelle Joyce. **155, 185** © HMCo./Allan Landau.

Illustration

87 Toby Williams. **112-113** Lois Ehlert. **115–126** (borders) Eileen Hine. **130, 132, 133–154** Rosario Valderrama. **163, 184** Sherri Haab. **191** Mircea Catusanu. **217** Lizi Boyd.

America lives in the heart of
every man everywhere
who wishes to find a region
where he will be free
to work out his destiny
as he chooses.

– Woodrow Wilson

Four Freedoms Souvenir Sheet
These stamps portray the essence of the
Four Freedoms and express America's determination to be a nation in which the people
enjoy freedom from want, freedom from fear,
freedom of speech and freedom of religion.
Norman Rockwell captured the importance
of these values perfectly on these stamps
that were issued as a souvenir sheet in 1994.
The text accompanying the stamps says it
best: "From our doughboys in WW I to our
astronauts striding across the moon, Norman
Rockwell's artwork has captured America's
traditional values along with the characteristic
optimism of its people."

An American History Album

THE STORY OF THE UNITED STATES
TOLD THROUGH STAMPS

Michael Worek and Jordan Worek
With an essay *The Art of the Stamp* by Terrence W. McCaffrey

FIREFLY BOOKS

A FIREFLY BOOK

Published by Firefly Books Ltd. 2008

First printing

Publisher Cataloging-in-Publication Data (U.S.)
Worek, Michael.
      An American history album : the story of the
United States told through stamps / Michael Worek
and Jordan Worek.
[   ] p. : col. photos. ;   cm.
Includes bibliographical references and index.
Summary: A look at the history of the United States
through the eyes of the United States Postal Service,
focusing on the people, places, events and
accomplishments that have been commemorated
on postage stamps over the last 100 years.
ISBN-13: 978-1-55407-390-0
ISBN-10: 1-55407-390-1
1. United States – History.
2. Stamp collecting. I. Worek, Jordan. II. Title.
973 dc22 E178.3.W6745 2008

Published in the United States by
Firefly Books (U.S.) Inc.
P.O. Box 1338, Ellicott Station
Buffalo, New York 14205

Published in Canada by
Firefly Books Ltd.
66 Leek Crescent
Richmond Hill, Ontario L4B 1H1

The publisher gratefully acknowledges the financial
support for our publishing program by the Government
of Canada through the Book Publishing Industry
Development Program.

Cover and interior design by Bob Wilcox

Printed in China

RIGHT: **100th Anniversary
United States Postage Stamps**
This souvenir sheet was issued to comple-
ment the Centenary International Philatelic
Exhibition held in New York City in 1947.
The first two United States stamps – a five
cent featuring Benjamin Franklin and a ten
cent featuring George Washington – are
reproduced here 100 years after their
original date of issue.

PAGE 12: **Definitive Issue of 1922–1930**
Although this book is concerned with the
commemorative stamps issued by the
United States, this selection of stamps from
the definitive issue of 1922–1930 illustrates
the beauty of those stamps issued for
everyday use to pay the postage rate. A
definitive issue must represent the entire
country, the artwork must be clearly visible
and appealing in a small space and the
design must be able to last for years without
seeming tired or dated. This set of definitive stamps is particularly successful in
achieving all these objectives.

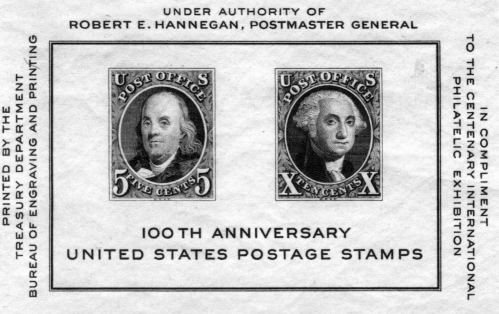

CONTENTS

THE WORLD'S MOST POPULAR HOBBY

In 1972, the United States issued a postage stamp honoring and promoting stamp collecting, the world's most popular hobby. The design featured the U.S. Post Office Department's first stamp, the five-cent issue of 1847, under a magnifying glass. This simple design illustrates how the hobby of stamp collecting is made even more fascinating when you know the stories behind the stamps. Behind that 1847 stamp is a story of exploration and national growth. By the

middle of the 19th century, along with steady immigration from Europe and the relentless push into western frontiers, the emergence of thriving industrial and commercial centers, war with Mexico, ideological conflict over slavery and sectional tension all demanded modernization of the expanding nation's postal service. Post Office customers and administrators alike recognized the need for postage stamps that could pay the cost of sending a letter anywhere in the country and even overseas. Andrew Jackson was briefly considered as the subject of that first stamp, but James B. Longacre's engraving of Benjamin Franklin, patriot and America's first postmaster, was selected because officials hoped it would be a unifying symbol for the deeply divided nation.

The 1847 stamp tells but one of many philatelic stories. The United States Post Office has since issued more than four thousand stamps, each one reflecting and shaping the ways the nation views its past. The subjects chosen, the style of the graphic elements, the shape, size, color and paper used, as well as the printing method employed and the means of separating individual stamps have all changed over time. Each era of stamp design has its own "feel," dictated in part by the image that postal and government leaders wish to project.

In *An American History Album*, the authors use stamps to illustrate the stories that make up American history in a visually exciting way. They show how, through great accomplishments and challenges, the American identity has changed over time. They have brought new life to United States history and to the stamps themselves by celebrating the nation's people, places, nature, events and culture. They have done what all collectors love to do: they have shared their album of stamps and stories with others.

Why do millions of people find joy in their stamp collections? Viewing, owning, researching and preserving these miniature art treasures brings pleasure and relaxation. Collectors can appreciate the social side of the hobby and actively join clubs or exhibit their collections at stamp shows. They can tailor their stamp collection to their interests and celebrate the things that are important to them. Some collectors search for stamps by country; others by topics such as lighthouses, golf, birds, or their home state. As you read this book, I hope that you too will find joy in the beauty of these stamps and the stories that they tell.

Cheryl R. Ganz, Ph. D.
Chief Curator of Philately
Smithsonian National Postal Museum

INTRODUCTION

Throughout its history, the United States has celebrated its achievements, honored its heroes and recorded its history by issuing commemorative postage stamps. These stamps tell us about the discovery and settlement of the land; advances in transportation and communication; wonders of the natural landscape; and accomplishments of political, military and civic leaders who served the republic and shaped its future. Created by the United States Post Office in the belief that the nation would be stronger for a tribute that combined historical significance with popular appeal, these stamps offer us a unique and proud look at America's history. The stamps are beautiful in themselves, but they take on even more interest when we learn the stories behind them – why they were issued, and who or what they honor. Taken together, these miniature works of art, created by some of the best artists and engravers of their day, constitute an American family album – a visual portrait of who we are, what we value and what we have accomplished.

Within the American colonies, letters were carried long before there were stamps to put on them. A post office was opened in Boston as early as 1639, and regular service between Boston and New York City began in 1673. Since its formation in 1775, the United States Post Office, originally called the Post Office Department, has been a key element in the nation's communication system and in the delivery of goods across the country and around the world. The world's first postage stamp, the famous Penny Black, was issued in England in 1840. The United States issued its first stamps in 1847. By 1850 every major country was using adhesive stamps to cover the postage rate, and letters were routinely mailed around the world with the assumption that they would arrive safely. In the United States registered mail was introduced in 1855, city delivery in 1874, and the first postcards, the emails of their day, in 1873.

It is clearly not the purpose here to recount the full story of the United States and its place in the world. That huge task is well beyond the scope of this little book or the postage stamps themselves. There are many excellent works that look judiciously at the American experience and give a balanced and reasoned picture of the nation's history, warts and all. Happily, with this book we are free to give ourselves over to the enjoyment of the high points, the best days, the most noble acts and the moments of courage, sacrifice and greatness that will always be remembered and associated with the country's history.

Like any family album, this one contains pictures only of the people and places we're proud of. They illustrate America's most patriotic perspective on its history. If at times, in this post-9/11 world, these images seem overly idealistic, we might remember that ideals often inspire our achievements. Those who have had the job of selecting, designing and issuing these little portraits of greatness have set a commendably high standard for illustrating our values and what we would like to become.

The selection of stamps in this book is notable as much for what has been omitted as for the stamps that have been included. The United States has just too many stories and too many commemorative stamps – more than four thousand in all – to show more than a fraction of them here. Stamps were selected for their subject matter – American history – and the beauty of their design as well as on the basis of the authors' personal views and preferences. Although chosen to reflect the themes of the book, they also represent some of the best work of the United States Post Office. Since so many more stamps have been issued than are presented here, and since most are still available from stamp dealers at a reasonable cost, we encourage readers to form their own collections of original Americana featuring their favorite themes and topics and, while they are at it, to learn more about our history.

As we move further into the electronic age of continuous communication with people everywhere, the postage stamps we have, and those that will be issued in the future, will remain as reminders of the pleasure we still experience in receiving a letter, in knowing that someone has taken the time to sit down and create a tangible bond between us. Unlike an email, a letter is a physical piece of history that we can read, treasure and pass down to our children. Appropriately, the stamps that have been issued to carry those letters are also worth treasuring, and surely a heritage to be enjoyed.

These stamps and the stories they tell are important because American history is important. The American experience, sometimes called "the last best hope of mankind," is one worth sharing because it is a story in which we all have a stake. More than thirty years ago, English journalist and broadcaster Alistair Cooke justified his efforts to create a television series about the United States by saying that whether he was to succeed or fail, it seemed to him a good, though difficult, thing "to try and say what is moving about the American experience ... at a time when that experience is either forgotten, badly taught, or shamelessly sentimentalized."

Cooke's words are still true today and justify any attempt, including this small one, to explore the best of America's aspirations and achievements. The United States is still poorly understood, even by many of its own citizens, but there is evidence in these stamps that the country is unique, resilient and somehow special. For all our rush into the future, history reminds us that the greatest good for the greatest number is best achieved by asking, with John F. Kennedy, not what your country can do for you, but what you can do for your country. These small tributes to the ideals, sacrifices and triumphs of the United States were created to help us take pride in the nation's history so that tomorrow's challenges may be faced with a surety of purpose and a confidence based on more than 200 years of experience in creating and sharing the American dream.

NOTE TO THE READER

This book covers only a small portion of our history and the postage stamps issued to commemorate it. More than 4,000 postage stamps have been issued to record and celebrate more than 500 years of history on this continent. Readers who wish to explore American history on its postage stamps further should begin with the Smithsonian National Postal Museum in Washington, D.C. The museum is devoted to presenting the colorful and engaging history of the nation's mail service and showcasing the largest and most comprehensive collection of stamps and philatelic material in the world. The museum is located at 2 Massachusetts Ave. N.E., across from Union Station. For more information visit the museum's Web site at www.postalmuseum.si.edu.

There are literally thousands of books on American history readily available as well as a wealth of original documents that sometimes prove more fascinating and readable than the books about them. A few books are listed in the Further Reading section at the end of this book. One of the most enjoyable and easily readable is *Alistair Cooke's America*, originally written in the 1970s as part of an ambitious BBC effort to celebrate the 200th anniversary of American independence.

The success of the American experiment is summed up in the words of Tony Blair, British Prime Minister from 1997 to 2007: "We are the ally of the U.S. not because they are powerful, but because we share their values. I am not surprised by anti-Americanism; but it is a foolish indulgence. For all their faults, and all nations have them, the U.S. are a force for good; they have liberal and democratic traditions of which any nation can be proud. I sometimes think it is a good rule of thumb to ask of a country: are people trying to get into it or out of it? It's not a bad guide to what sort of country it is." By the Prime Minister's standard, the last 400 years of immigration stand as irrefutable testimony to the success of the America Dream.

Religious Freedom and Freedom of the Press
These two stamps celebrate the importance Americans have placed, since the very first days of our nation, on the right of each citizen to freedom of the press and freedom of religion.

The crisis we are facing today ...
requires our willingness to believe
in our capacity to perform
great deeds ... and, after all,
why shouldn't we believe that?
We are Americans.

– Ronald Reagan

PART 1

HERITAGE
AND
VALUES

HERITAGE AND VALUES

America has always been known for its compassion, idealism and concern for human rights. From its earliest settlement, America opened its doors to oppressed and persecuted people from around the world. The words engraved at the base of the Statue of Liberty, a gift to the United States from France in honor of the friendship between the two countries, express the hope for a new and better life that motivated millions of immigrants, including those who arrived long before the statue, to make the difficult and dangerous journey to a new and unknown land:

> *"Keep, ancient lands, your storied pomp!" cries she*
> *with silent lips. "Give me your tired, your poor,*
> *Your huddled masses yearning to breathe free,*
> *The wretched refuse of your teeming shore.*
> *Send these, the homeless, tempest-tossed to me.*
> *I lift my lamp beside the golden door."*

From the Pilgrims in 1620 to the millions of poor, homeless and "tempest-tossed" immigrants who came to these shores in the more than 250 years before the Statue of Liberty was created, and to those who have followed them in the 130 years since then, America has always been more than just a country. "Going to America" has been the dream of the world's poor and dispossessed for a better life, a life of opportunity, education and freedom – a life in a place that gives all citizens a chance to reach their full potential and be the best they can be.

One of the things that characterizes America, often to the consternation of the rest of the world, is the nation's patriotism and the pride its citizens take in their country and their heritage. Perhaps the reason Americans are so willing to express their patriotism, to wear their heart on their sleeve so to speak, is that the United States has always attached a great deal of importance to freedom of speech, freedom of religion, and freedom from fear – ideals written into the Constitution itself. Indeed, America is unique in being a country that was founded not on the basis of geography, or race, or history or accident, but on a set of beliefs that the Founding Fathers found "self-evident" and for which they were prepared to fight and die.

A few of the stamps issued over the years to remind us of our heritage and the value we place on our nation, our history, our land and our leaders are shown on the next few pages. The Credo stamps represent the great American heritage of respect not only for our values and beliefs but also for the value of values themselves. As a nation we have preserved many sayings from great Americans that remind us of the basic creed of our freedom, and these words still form the basis of who we are and how we think. The numerous stamps showing the flag are among the best demonstrations of Americans' pride in standing up for what they believe in. The flag is flown proudly everywhere from the White House to millions of small front porches across the country.

America was determined to avoid the religious persecutions that had driven so many settlers to its shores. The Founding Fathers demanded freedom of religious thought and practice – or no practice at all – as a basic right for all citizens. Nevertheless, a respect for religion and a belief in God, however worshiped, has characterized our nation from George Washington to George Bush. We are, as the Pledge of Allegiance so eloquently says, "one nation, under God" and the dollar still proclaims, directly over the eagle clutching arrows in its talons, "In God We Trust."

Washington, D.C., is unique among American cities. Although monuments to local heroes abound in cities and towns across the country, here in the capital the nation's greatest collection of public buildings, monuments and treasures is to be found. As the beauty of these stamps shows, Washington is a capital city truly worthy of a great nation.

As a nation we have been richly blessed. The preservation and transmission of our faith and values to the next generation in a world increasingly cynical and self-absorbed, remains perhaps the most important task before us.

Long May It Wave

Of all America's symbols, none is more famous, more loved or more commonly seen than its flag. Drive through any city or town in the United States and you will find flags flying proudly on houses, businesses, schools and public buildings everywhere. So closely identified is the flag with all that the country stands for that one of the most prominent images of our time, shown on the 25th Anniversary of the First Moon Landing stamp, is of astronaut James Irwin saluting the flag with the lunar rover in the background.

The first American flag was authorized by an Act of Congress on June 14, 1777, in a resolution that states: "the flag of the United States be thirteen stripes, alternate red and white; that the union be thirteen stars, white in a blue field, representing a new constellation." The new flag provided a much-needed symbol of unity and determination for the young nation still struggling to be born.

In 1794 Congress authorized a flag with 15 stars and 15 stripes to recognize the addition of Vermont and Kentucky to the Union. In 1818 Congress established the design of the flag we now have, 13 stripes and an addition of one star for each state added to the Union, with new stars to be added on the July 4th following the admission of the new state.

For much of the 20th century, after Arizona was admitted to the Union in 1912, the flag carried 48 stars. The stamp bearing the date July 4, 1959, shows the short-lived 49-star flag that was in use between the admission of Alaska as the 49th state on January 3, 1959, and the admission of Hawaii as the 50th state on August 21, 1959.

A large and defiant American flag that was still flying proudly over Baltimore's Fort McHenry after a British bombardment lasting 25 hours inspired "The Star-Spangled Banner," originally written in 1814 as a poem by Francis Scott Key. That actual flag survived and is now in the Smithsonian Institution in Washington, D.C.

In 1949 President Truman signed an Act of Congress designating June 14th as National Flag Day. The Pledge of Allegiance was officially recognized by Congress in 1942, and in 1954 an amendment was made to add the words "under God" to give us the Pledge of Allegiance we now know. In words that echo those of so many of the Founding Fathers, President Eisenhower said of adding the words "under God" to the Pledge: "In this way we are reaffirming the transcendence of religious faith in America's heritage and future; in this way we shall constantly strengthen those spiritual weapons which forever will be our country's most powerful resource in peace and war." This ubiquitous symbol has stood for the nation virtually since its inception. Long may it wave.

I Pledge allegiance to the Flag
of the United States of America
and to the Republic for which it stands,
one Nation, under God, indivisible,
with Liberty and Justice for all.

The White House

USA 33

2000

Monument to the Nation

In 1776 the delegates to the Second Continental Congress met in Philadelphia, Pennsylvania, and signed the Declaration of Independence. In 1787 the Constitutional Convention met again in Philadelphia to draft the Constitution. Philadelphia, a major city at the approximate center of the thirteen colonies, was a logical place to meet but it was not destined to become the permanent capital of the new nation.

Article 1, Section 8, Clause 17 of the Constitution provided for a national capital outside the jurisdiction of any of the states. It provided Congress itself with the authority "to exercise exclusive Legislation in all Cases whatsoever, over such District (not exceeding ten Miles square) as may, by Cession of particular States, and the Acceptance of Congress, become the Seat of the Government of the United States."

Both Maryland and Virginia offered land along the

Potomac River in 1790, and President Washington selected the present site for the capital on land taken from Maryland north of the river and from Virginia south of the river. Major Pierre L'Enfant, a French artist and engineer who had served with Washington in the Revolutionary War, designed the new city. The plan featured a grid system overlaid with diagonal avenues that radiated from the two most important buildings in the city – the President's House and the building that would house Congress.

The government officially moved to the new City of Washington, named after the President, in the District of Columbia, in December 1800. Only one wing of the Capitol was completed and the President's House was still under construction. Building proceeded slowly in what was still largely wilderness, but the city's population grew to about 24,000 in 1810. During the War of

1812, the British invaded and burned the President's House, the Capitol and other public buildings, requiring them all to be rebuilt. In 1846 Congress determined that it did not need the land south of the Potomac and returned title to the land to the state of Virginia.

Washington residents were only allowed to vote in Presidential elections with the passing of the 23rd Amendment to the Constitution in 1961. In 1992 the House of Representatives passed a measure approving statehood for the District, but the Senate refused to consider it. The District of Columbia is still governed directly by Congress without local representation.

Millions of tourists from around the world visit Washington each year, and L'Enfant's basic design remains largely in place today. The buildings in the capital as we know it are a result of the work of the McMillan Plan devised by a Congressional Committee

formed in 1901 and composed of some of the greatest Americans ever involved in city planning. These included Daniel Burnham, who had been instrumental in the World's Columbian Exposition in Chicago in 1892, landscape architect Frederick Law Olmsted, Jr., architect Charles F. McKim, and sculptor Augustus Saint-Gaudens. Their work resulted in the beautiful city we know today, designed around the Mall with monuments and views in every direction.

President Theodore Roosevelt authorized "The White House" as the official name for the President's residence in 1901. It now ranks among the most famous buildings in the world and is instantly recognizable to millions around the world. The $3.50 stamp showing the dome of the Capitol paid the Priority Mail rate. The high value $12.25 issue showing the Washington Monument and the Reflecting Pool paid the Express Mail rate.

Office of the President

The President of the United States is widely considered the most powerful political figure in the world today. Both the person and the office command enormous respect around the world, if for no other reason than that so much of the world's trade and security is linked directly to the economic and foreign policy of the United States.

The President is the chief executive officer of the Federal Government and the Commander-in-Chief of the Armed Forces. He appoints diplomatic representatives, Supreme Court judges and many other officials; initiates the greatest number of legislative proposals that become law; has the power of veto over legislation passed by Congress; and can issue executive orders that have the force of law.

But perhaps the President's greatest influence stems not from these powers but from the fact that the President holds the only elected position in the nation for which every citizen can vote. Every other elected representative in Washington has only to represent his or her local constituents. The President, however, must represent everyone in the country. From this wide power base comes very extensive authority to speak for the people and the nation as a whole. In making any decision, therefore, the President faces enormous pressure from various regional and political interests. He or she must try to be fair to all segments of this sprawling nation as well as take into account the influence that any legislation or policy will have on countries around the world.

At the inaugural ceremony the newly elected President takes a very short oath of office: "I do solemnly swear that I will faithfully execute the Office of President of the United States, and will to the best of my ability, preserve, protect and defend the Constitution of the United States." This simple oath, which firmly anchors the Office of the President to the Constitution, is the fundamental statement of how this nation is to be governed.

Until the election of Franklin D. Roosevelt for a third term in 1940 and then for a fourth term in 1944, American presidents had limited themselves, by tradition going back to George Washington, to two terms in office. In 1951 the Twenty-Second Amendment to the Constitution specifically forbids anyone from being elected president more than twice and, in the event that a president has served two or more years of a predecessor's term, he or she may only be elected for a single additional term.

Between 1789 and 2007 there have been 43 presidents. Nine presidents since 1900 have been elected more than once: Theodore Roosevelt, Woodrow Wilson, Franklin D. Roosevelt, Harry Truman, Dwight Eisenhower, Richard Nixon, Ronald Reagan, William Clinton and George W. Bush. Four presidents have died in office: William Henry Harrison (1841), Zachary Taylor (1850), Warren G. Harding (1923) and Franklin D. Roosevelt (1945). Four presidents have been assassinated: Abraham Lincoln (1865), James A. Garfield (1881),

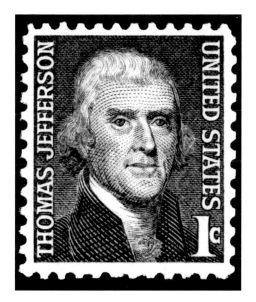

Harry S. Truman

U.S. Postage 8 cents

U.S. 6c POSTAGE

DWIGHT D.
EISENHOWER

William McKinley (1901) and John F. Kennedy (1963). Only one president has resigned – Richard Nixon in 1974, over the Watergate scandal.

The influence of the President has often outlived the man. Some memorable presidential statements still guide us today. George Washington, in his Farewell Address, warned the young nation "to keep the United States free from political connections with every other country." Although our power and influence now make such independence impossible, this isolationist sentiment is one to which a large number of Americans still subscribe. Abraham Lincoln warned the South in his Inaugural Address that we citizens,

and not the President, would have to find the solution to our sectional differences: "In your hands, my dissatisfied fellow countrymen, and not in mine, is the momentous issue of civil war."

This advice – to value what we have as a nation and to do everything we can to preserve it – was echoed a century later by John F. Kennedy in his Inaugural Address when he reminded another generation of Americans: "In your hands, my fellow citizens, more than in mine, will rest the final success or failure of our course." And, in a more personal way, he reminded citizens of America and of the world to look to service and not entitlement: "And so, my

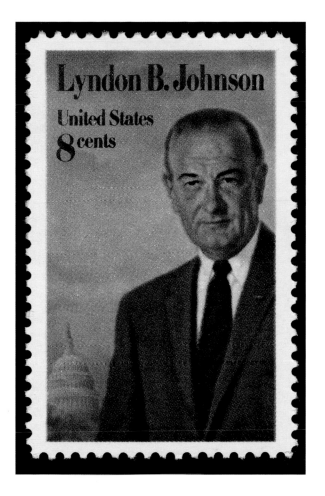

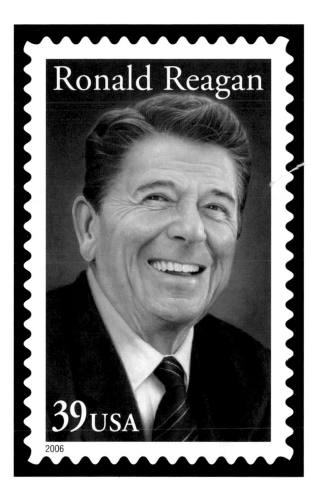

fellow Americans: ask not what your country can do for you – ask what you can do for your country. My fellow citizens of the world: ask not what America will do for you, but what together we can do for the freedom of man."

Dwight Eisenhower, the foremost American military mind since Washington, warned in his Valedictory Address that victory in war could endanger our liberty in times of peace: "This conjunction of an immense military establishment and a large arms industry is new in the American experience. The total influence – economic, political, even spiritual – is felt in every city, every State house, every office of the Federal Government. We recognize the imperative need for this development. Yet we must not fail to comprehend its grave implications . . . we must guard against the acquisition of unwarranted influence, whether sought or unsought, by the military/industrial complex. The potential for the disastrous rise of misplaced power exists and will persist."

Although individual presidents, like all of us, have sometimes failed to live up to what was expected of them, the office itself carries with it so much temporal and moral authority that, overall during the past two centuries, it has delivered all that the Founding Fathers could have hoped from it.

Words to Live By

These Credo stamps celebrate some of the words of wisdom that have been most important in guiding the nation since its inception. Although these sayings reach back 200 years, each contains some good council that we would do well to heed today.

Patrick Henry's "Give me liberty or give me death," see the stamp on page 36, became a rallying cry during the earliest days of the American Revolution. The words are the concluding sentence of a passionate speech Henry made on March 23, 1775, urging the colony of Virginia to join with Massachusetts and the other colonies already engaged in armed resistance to the British. Although the words quoted on this stamp are the most famous, the last three sentences of Henry's speech are also worth remembering: "Is life so dear, or peace so sweet, as to be purchased at the price of chains and slavery? Forbid it, Almighty God! I know not what course others may take; but as for me, give me liberty, or give me death!"

Thomas Jefferson's words, contained in a private letter written in 1800, are a passionate defense of intellectual freedom. Jefferson was one of the outstanding minds of his time and a man who fervently believed in people's ability to think for themselves and to govern themselves. The complete sentence from which these words are taken reads "I have sworn upon the altar of God eternal hostility against every form of tyranny over the mind of man."

Benjamin Franklin's simple but effective words, "Fear to do ill, and you need fear Nought else," are typical of the wit and wisdom that secures Franklin's hold on the American imagination to this day. Franklin began publishing his *Poor Richard's Almanack* in 1733. Along with weather forecasts, tide tables and the position of the moon, it contained hundreds of wise maxims that helped shape the thinking and values of the colonies.

The last quotation from the Revolutionary War period, "Observe good faith and justice toward all nations," comes from George Washington's Farewell Address at the end of his second term as president in 1796. Washington was a firm believer in the doctrine that the United States should deal fairly and equally with all nations and have preferential relations with none. Later in the address he puts forward his view of American foreign policy: "The great rule of conduct for us in regard to foreign nations is, in extending our commercial relations to have with them as little political connection as possible."

Abraham Lincoln's words, contained in a private letter to Henry Pierce written in 1859, clearly express his belief in the necessity for a free people to respect the freedom of others. The complete sentence from which this quotation is taken reads: "This is a world of compensations; and he who would be no slave, must consent to have no slave. Those who deny freedom to others, deserve it not for themselves; and, under a just God, can not long retain it."

Francis Scott Key's words "And this be our Motto, in GOD is our TRUST," written in 1814, come, of course, from the poem that was to become the American national anthem, "The Star-Spangled Banner." It expresses the close link between the well-being of the country and its faith in God that was so characteristic of those who led our nation at the time of its formation.

The Declaration of Independence

With this document began eight long years of war during which thirteen small colonies, joined together in a loose union, raised a small army to fight against the most powerful nation in the world. Not many in Europe could have given them much chance for success. Yet the bold language and bold signatures on this parchment show that belief in the rightness of their action and the justness of their cause gave them a confidence to match their passion. By signing, circulating and preserving this document each man stood convicted of high treason against the Crown. That they understood the gravity of their actions is clear from Patrick Henry's famous line, uttered in the Virginia legislature: "Give me liberty or give me death." For the signators of the Declaration of Independence these were now the only two choices available and that knowledge must have strengthened their resolve to fight on during the long and difficult war ahead. The Declaration of Independence was approved by the Continental Congress on July 4th but not actually written out and signed until August 2, 1776. This stamp was issued in 1961.

Philadelphia Sesquicentennial Exposition

Perhaps second only to the flag, the Liberty Bell is the most famous American symbol. The bell was ordered by Pennsylvania in 1751 to celebrate the 50th anniversary of William Penn's original constitution for the colony issued in 1701. During the Revolutionary War British troops occupied Philadelphia in 1777. A few weeks before the arrival of the British, all the bells in the city had been taken down and removed to prevent the British from melting them down to make cannon. The Liberty Bell was hidden in Zion Reformed Church in Allentown, Pennsylvania. After the Revolution, the bell was used by anti-slavery advocates, and later by those advocating women's suffrage, as a symbol of freedom for those whose rights had been passed over in the drafting of the Constitution itself. After the Civil War, the bell was frequently displayed at major exhibitions around the country to promote unity and patriotism in the nation. In 1926, to celebrate the 150th anniversary of the Declaration of Independence

and the birth of America, an exposition was held in Philadelphia. The giant replica of the Liberty Bell suspended above the road leading to the exhibition grounds is shown in this picture as the presidential motorcade passes underneath. The stamp was released on May 10, 1926, and features an image of the liberty bell replica constructed for the exposition rather than the original that hangs in Philadelphia.

With Liberty and Justice for All

The words of Dr. Martin Luther King Jr. "that all men, yes, black men as well as white men, would be guaranteed the unalienable rights of life, liberty and the pursuit of happiness" echoed through the 1960s. Although slavery ended with the Civil War, true equality remained a dream for black Americans for another 100 years. The stamps shown here honor the cause of freedom and equality for all Americans.

The rights of Hispanic Americans, women, Native Americans, Black Americans and many other minorities were all earned only after long struggle.

Sojourner Truth, an early speaker and writer against slavery, was born a slave in 1797. She lived long enough to urge black men to fight for the Union in the Civil War and be received at the White House by President Lincoln. A. Philip Randolph, the founder of the Brotherhood of Sleeping Car Porters, believed that the future for black Americans lay in good jobs as well as civil rights. He led campaigns for an end to segregation in the labor unions and in the military and organized the 1963 March on Washington for Jobs and Freedom. Whitney Moore Young, head of the National Urban League for a decade, is credited with persuading American business leaders to support the civil rights movement. Thurgood Marshall, the first black American to sit on the Supreme Court, worked tirelessly for affirmative action programs and an end to segregation.

National Parks Centennial

Mount McKinley · Alaska

U.S. 15c

Protecting the Wilderness

It was the availability of natural resources in the wilderness that determined the success of early European settlement in the New World. In Central and South America the presence of gold and silver formed the basis of the earliest colonial settlement and exploration. In Canada the abundance of beaver, coupled with the European demand for furs, was responsible for establishing the fur trade and the exploration of much of the continent by canoe. In the United States, blessed with more familiar and hospitable climates than the lands to the north or south, the first colonial economies and trade with Britain and Europe were based on agricultural products and timber.

In the era before the Industrial Revolution, wealth was still based on land and the majority of people lived and worked on farms. The land, however, was neither inexhaustible in quantity or fertility. The earliest settlers in New England had found that once the forest cover was removed, the soil proved thin, and the first – sometimes the only – crop they could grow was rocks. Plantation owners in the south found that cotton and tobacco quickly depleted the soil and, being too impatient to let fields lie fallow and recover, pushed farther west and south in search of new lands to exploit. By the end of the Civil War, the lands east of the Mississippi had been occupied; great forests

and abundant wildlife there were already becoming a thing of memory.

In the West the plowing of the great plains reduced the natural cover of the land and by the 1930s the soil blew away in great clouds creating a "dust bowl" that drove thousands of small farmers off the exhausted land. The government introduced programs to pay farmers to take land out of production as well as offering education and regulatory programs designed to prevent more damage.

The emphasis gradually shifted from farming to discovering and exploiting the oil, gas, minerals and precious metals that lay beneath the surface. The industrial age had turned once lovely villages into packed industrial cities and created the first stirrings of nostalgia for wilderness. Faced with the grim reality of overcrowding, dirt and noise in the cities, Americans began to turn their attention to preserving what wilderness and natural beauty remained.

The first national park, Yellowstone, was created to preserve one of the few unexplored regions left in the west. In 1872 President Grant signed a bill establishing the area as a "great national park or pleasure-ground for the benefit and enjoyment of the people."

Other parks soon followed, and by the end of World War I a total of 13 national parks had been

created. Most were in the west, but some significant national forests were preserved in the east as well as much of the Everglades in Florida. State parks soon followed and although logging and mineral exploration were often permitted, some prime examples of wilderness had at least been saved.

More than 10 million Americans visit today's National Parks System every year. Visitors from around the world come determined to experience wilderness on a grand scale no longer available in the crowded countries of Europe and Asia. Mount Rushmore National Memorial alone receives three million visitors a year. Busts of Washington, Jefferson, Theodore Roosevelt and Lincoln are carved in granite amid the beauty of the Black Hills.

The decision to preserve our wilderness through national and state parks marked a historic turning point in our thinking. We began gradually moving away from considering the land as a possession to be exploited for personal gain and toward seeing it as an inheritance of which we have been given temporary custody, and for which we are responsible before we hand it down to our children.

Today, more and more Americans seem willing to tread lightly on the earth and set strict limits on the use of our natural resources to ensure the survival of our wilderness heritage.

Wildlife Conservation

Among the first recorded impressions of the natural wonders of the New World are the accounts of early European fishermen on the Grand Banks off Newfoundland. They told with amazement of cod so plentiful that you could almost walk on their backs across the water and arrive on land without getting your feet wet. While it was an exaggeration, it did give a sense of the wealth that awaited those early settlers – mature forests of magnificent trees that formed vast natural cathedrals, their trunks like pillars supporting the green canopy overhead; buffalo herds so immense that travelers had to wait all day for them to pass; and, as John James Audubon recorded, such endless flocks of pigeons that the "air was literally filled … the light of noon-day was obscured as by an eclipse … and the continued buzz of wings had a tendency to lull my senses to repose … the pigeons were still passing in undiminished numbers … for three days in succession." Given such bounty, it seemed as if the natural resources of this vast land were truly inexhaustible.

But, as settlers soon learned, the natural resources of the continent were far from inexhaustible. As early as

the 1630s the New England colonies were regulating hunting, fishing and the cutting of timber. The pressure on wildlife and the land itself increased dramatically as the population of the nation exploded from some 5 million in 1800 to almost 80 million by 1900.

Market hunting in marshes and wetlands became a highly profitable business. Hunters could kill hundreds of birds at a time just by firing huge shotguns into the flocks, and after the arrival of the railway in the 1850s, millions of birds were shipped annually from the Great Lakes area to meat markets in the east. Their great numbers and low cost made them easy and attractive prey. Buffalo herds came close to extinction for the same reason. No hunting was required; they were easy to find and kill to feed the gangs of men working on the railroads being built across the nation. As a result of such mass slaughters, only 800 bison remained by 1900 and the last passenger pigeon died in captivity in 1914.

Soil conservation was a lesson learned the hard way. On the prairies, the abundant grass that had protected the land was plowed for farming. Cattle and sheep were also allowed to overgraze, thus destroying the natural vegetation. Left unprotected, the soil blew away on the wind, especially in drought conditions. Water conservation initially focused on preventing flooding and silting up of rivers and harbors, but

since the middle of the 20th century efforts have been directed toward reducing pollution and improving waste treatment to preserve clean water.

Ironically, it was wealthy hunters and sportsmen, and not conservationists, who first demanded regulations on market hunting and the protection of wetlands and breeding grounds. They wanted to ensure unlimited game for future hunting and sport. The New York Sporting Club, opened in 1844, soon became the New York State Game Protective Society. In 1905, with the encouragement of President Theodore Roosevelt, himself a keen sportsman and conservationist, Congress created the United States Forest Service to administer a new system of protected forests and national parks.

In 1918 the *Migratory Bird Treaty Act* for the protection of birds that summered in Canada and wintered in the United States was passed. Duck stamps were begun in 1934; duck hunters were charged a small fee that was used to protect habitat and ensure a supply of ducks for the future. In 1940 the United States Fish and Wildlife Service was formed.

Our endangered species today are perhaps less dramatic than the passenger pigeon and buffalo of the past, but they are no less important; for all are part of the great interconnected web of life on which humanity depends.

Endangered Species

National Stamp Collecting Month 1996 highlights these 15 species to promote awareness of endangered wildlife. Each generation must work to protect the delicate balance of nature, so that future generations may share a sound and healthy planet.

John Fitzgerald Kennedy

The Presidency of John Fitzgerald Kennedy was tragically cut short with his assassination in Dallas, Texas, on November 22, 1963. In the few years he held office, Kennedy presided over the nation at one of the most dangerous moments in the Cold War – the Cuban Missile Crisis. In his Inaugural Address he had expressed the nation's willingness to "pay any price, bear any burden, meet any hardship" to preserve its liberty. America's obvious willingness to live up to those words was sufficient deterrent to get the missiles withdrawn and preserve the peace. But Kennedy, like the best and most effective presidents, made his greatest contribution to the nation by giving Americans hope for the future. The youngest man elected to office, the first Catholic and the man with the polished and beautiful wife and children, Kennedy symbolized the dream of the postwar generation that had grown up with the Depression and then been "tempered by war, disciplined by a hard and bitter peace" for security and prosperity with a purpose.

His words, "ask not what your country can do for you, ask what you can do for your country," gave birth to an optimism and pride in ourselves and our country that would be tragically shattered with his death. This photograph taken on May 25, 1962, shows John Kennedy Jr. playing under the President's desk. The stamp features the eternal flame that burns at his grave in Arlington National Cemetery. It was issued on May 29, 1964.

46

The World Trade Center, New York City

No event in recent American history has had greater impact on American thinking about their position in the world and their vulnerability than the terrorist attack on New York and Washington on the morning of September 11, 2001. Although the Pentagon was badly damaged, the image that will always be associated with the day that war came home to American soil is the destruction of the Twin Towers in New York. This photograph shows the towers soaring over Manhattan on May 6, 1980. Constructed in 1972 at a cost of $400 million, each 110-story tower was 1,368 feet high and required over 100 elevators to move the thousands of people who used the buildings each day. These proud symbols of America's economic strength were struck by two commercial airliners traveling at more than 400 miles per hour. Within minutes of impact the fully loaded aircraft fuel tanks had started a fire of such heat and intensity that the steel structure of the building eventually weakened to the point that the buildings collapsed floor by floor while the eyes of the world watched on television. More than 2,800 people died in the attack including more than 343 New York firemen and paramedics who entered the doomed buildings in an attempt to save lives. This stamp, issued on June 7, 2002, shows the devastation and the raising of an American flag in defiance of the enemy; it is an image of heroism and vulnerability that will remain forever etched in the American conscience.

For this is what America is all about,
it is the uncrossed desert
and the unclimbed ridge,
it is the star that is not reached
and the harvest that is sleeping
in the unplowed ground.

– Lyndon Johnson

PART 2

DISCOVERY
AND
EXPLORATION

DISCOVERY AND EXPLORATION

Almost as soon as it was discovered by Europeans, the New World in general and the United States in particular became a symbol of the physical and spiritual adventure upon which all humanity is engaged. The physical adventure of coming to America spoke of people's willingness to leave behind every familiar thing, to take great risks and subject themselves to enormous hardship for the sake of a better life for themselves and their children. The spiritual adventure has played itself out in the way each generation of American immigrants has thrived under the protection of their inalienable right to life, liberty and the pursuit of happiness.

Some newcomers were Puritans or members of other religious groups who wished to build a little bit of heaven here on earth; some were philosophers determined to try bold new experiments of government; some were criminals who came to escape justice in their native land; others were lazy opportunists looking for new lands and people to exploit and plunder. But all these immigrants have believed one thing: no matter what their goal, they stood a better chance of success in America than in any other country.

As John Winthrop, leader of the English Puritans who settled Massachusetts Bay Colony in 1630, predicted, their quest for the American dream would be carefully watched by the entire world. "For we must consider that we shall be as a city upon a hill, the eyes of all people are upon us. So that if we shall deal falsely with our god in this work we have undertaken, and so cause him to withdraw his present help from us, we shall be made a story and a byword throughout the world."

The Puritans would indeed be a city on a hill, a lamp to light the path of millions of others around the world that would also see in America the chance to realize their dreams. Unlike the little band of Pilgrims who had preceded them, the Puritans were numerous, ambitious and organized – determined to succeed financially as well as spiritually. Between 1630 and 1642 over 20,000 Puritans left England and settled in Massachusetts Bay Colony. Considering that the entire population of the English colonies in 1650 numbered only a little over 50,000, it is not surprising that this huge influx of like-minded people with determination and clarity of purpose left such a strong mark on the American character.

American history begins with Columbus's voyage in 1492. For almost 100 years after Columbus, Spain and Portugal had the New World and its riches largely to themselves. By 1540 Spanish explorers in search of gold had pushed north as far as California. Not realizing that the gold they sought was indeed there, they only established a few missions and forts before turning their attention to Mexico and South America. The gold would not be discovered for another 300 years – during the California Gold Rush, when the territory was already a part of the United States.

The French had been trading for furs in Canada since the 1530s. In 1608 they founded Quebec City and began to build a thinly settled but immense empire that would lay claim to Canada and the entire Mississippi River watershed. The first English attempt at settlement had taken place in 1585 but it was a failure. Not until 1607 was England able to establish a permanent colony at Jamestown. Once the English colonies were established, however, they possessed an immense advantage over French and Spanish settlements. The English had come to settle the land and establish towns and cities that would grow rapidly rather than just to establish trading ports and exploit the natural resources.

Struggle for control of the frontier between the English and the French went on with increasing intensity in the Ohio Valley. As with so much other American history during the early years, the question of who was to control the continent was settled in Europe. During the Seven Years' War, 1756–1763, Britain and Prussia were locked in a struggle for dominance on the European continent with France and Austria. Britain provided massive financial support to Prussia, whose soldiers were able to gain victory in Europe. With Prussia busy fighting in Europe, British troops had been able to defeat the French in the West Indies and had captured Quebec in 1759. Under the terms of the Treaty of Paris in 1763, no significant changes were made to the European boundaries, but the map of North America was dramatically redrawn. The British received all of Canada, the Ohio River Valley and the eastern half of the Mississippi River Valley.

Although the 13 English colonies had been confined by the French to a thin strip of land along the Atlantic coast from 1607 to 1763, they had grown in population, wealth and determination to control their future. The world was about to witness the explosion of American power as the 13 colonies first won their independence in 1783 and then, in the space of a single lifetime, gained possession of the entire continental United States only 65 years later in 1848. By 1893, as the World's Columbian Exposition celebrated the 400th anniversary of Columbus's discovery of the New World, the vast empty lands of the west had been settled and the frontier was declared officially closed. The discovery and exploration of America were complete.

For Gospel and for Gold

Christopher Columbus, born in Genoa in 1451, spent many years traveling to the courts of Europe trying to persuade kings and princes that it was possible and practical to sail west from Europe and reach the Indies. The goal was the lucrative trade in spices – pepper, cinnamon, cloves and nutmeg – that was available from China, India and Indonesia and in great demand in Europe. The spice trade from the east had flourished throughout the Middle Ages, but the Moors now controlled the overland route. Columbus's appeal for funds was based on his promise to re-establish this lucrative trade in the hands of Europeans.

Columbus was turned down on three different occasions by their Most Holy Catholic Majesties, King Ferdinand and Queen Isabella of Spain. Finally, in 1492, they agreed to back a single voyage of exploration. The voyage, their majesties hoped, would be "for gospel and for gold," as Columbus's commission so eloquently put it, establishing right from the start the twin passions of the next 200 years of exploration – religion and profit – and the tricky business of combining the two.

On August 3, 1492, Columbus left Spain. His little flagship, the *Santa Maria*, was only 119 feet long; the *Nina* and the *Pinta* were less than half that size, and

the three ships together carried only 104 men. After more than nine weeks at sea, with his crew on the verge of mutiny and wanting to turn back, they reached an island they named San Salvador in the Bahamas and then sailed on to Cuba. His ships had covered an average of 150 miles a day through completely uncharted waters, an astounding feat that attests to the seamanship of the early explorers, who would soon sail around the world and into every ocean without charts or communications of any kind.

The *Santa Maria* ran aground and was wrecked on Christmas Day, 1492. The limited space on the remaining ships meant that 40 men had to be left behind in a small fort on Cuba to await Columbus's return. Convinced that he had reached the Indies, Columbus set sail from Cuba in January, 1493, and returned to a hero's welcome in Spain. He was made "Admiral of the Ocean Sea" and governor of any further territory he might discover.

Columbus's second expedition, this time comprising more than 1,200 men in 17 ships, took three years. He found the little fort he had left behind destroyed, and all his men killed. He established the town of Santo Domingo and conquered the island of Cuba. Reports of his brutal treatment of the Indians and the colonists reached Spain, and Columbus, leaving his two brothers in charge, sailed back to Spain to answer the accusations. Two more expeditions followed. After the second, upon hearing reports of food shortages and unrest in the colonies, the Spanish monarchs sent a representative to investigate conditions in the New World. Columbus was sent home in chains in 1500. Although he was restored to favor and led a fourth and final voyage, he had lost control of his find and returned to Spain, where he died in obscurity in 1505. His voyages, however, mark the beginnings of American history.

Other great Spanish explorers soon began to enlarge on his discovery and captured an empire for Spain: Vasco Nunez de Balboa, Amerigo Vespucci (for whom America was named), Juan Ponce de León, Hernando Cortes, Francisco Vasquez de Coronado and Hernando de Soto are among the most famous.

These stamps are from the famous Columbian Exposition series issued in 1893 to mark the 400th Anniversary of Columbus's voyage. Clearly intended for collectors, high values, up to $5.00, had no real use in the payment of postage. Nevertheless, this series, the first American commemorative stamp issue, proved very popular and began the practice of commemorating American history on its postage stamps.

Founding of Jamestown

Central and South America, rich in gold but with a climate and soil largely unsuited to European agriculture, had yielded immense wealth for Spain. A desire to obtain a share of New World riches for itself led England to establish its first colonies in Virginia, a thousand miles to the north of Cuba.

In 1585 Sir Walter Raleigh founded a colony on Roanoke Island. The first settlers, 108 ill-equipped and unprepared men, were immediately in trouble with the Indians. Having exhausted their food supplies, they returned to England in 1586 with Sir Francis Drake, when he stopped at the colony on the way home to England after a successful raid on Spanish settlements in the West Indies. A second group of settlers arrived but left only 18 men; the rest returned to England. These men had all died by the time the third expedition, 117 men, women and children led by Governor John White, arrived the next summer in 1587. White too returned to England almost immediately and was not able to return to the little colony until 1590. When he arrived he found no trace of the settlers, who had died, wandered off into the wilderness or been killed or captured by the Indians. Although a failure in every way, the ill-fated colony has the distinction of being the first attempt at colonization by the English and the location of the birth of Virginia Dare, the first nonnative child born in North America.

The first successful English settlement was established at Jamestown. In 1606 James I of England granted a charter that gave the London Company rights to settle lands that ran from modern day North Carolina to New York and granted the Plymouth Company rights to settle lands in New England. In 1607 Captain John Smith sailed up the James River and established a colony in a malarial swamp surrounded by heavy forests, a position that he felt would be easy to defend. Like Roanoke, the colonists were ill suited for the work of carving a settlement out of wilderness. Unwilling or unable to do the backbreaking work, susceptible to malaria and other diseases and lacking food, fewer than 40 of the original 120 settlers survived the first year. Nine ships and 600 men and women left England for the colony in 1609. After hurricanes and shipwreck the settlers arrived only to succumb in turn to disease and starvation.

The remaining settlers were about to abandon the colony and return to England when a supply ship, commanded by Lord de la Warr, arrived at the mouth of the river. The little English settlement survived and slowly grew through immigration. It was a close call.

The five-cent stamp shown here depicts Pocahontas, the daughter of Chief Powhatan, who had enlisted the settlers into helping him in his battles with other tribes. Pocahontas met and married John Rolfe, a settler credited with the establishment of the tobacco crop in Virginia. Pocahontas converted to Christianity and returned to England with her husband. Tobacco eventually became the south's first source of wealth as well as its undoing. The labor required to grow tobacco in the subtropical climate was destined to be provided by black slaves. The first slave ship from Africa arrived in Virginia just 12 years after the little settlement was established.

A City Upon a Hill

The Pilgrims hold a unique place in American history and mythology, despite their small number and short history. Unlike the majority of immigrants to America, the Pilgrims did not come to make a more prosperous life for themselves, or to convert the natives to Christianity, or for gold, or for the glory of King and Country. They came, simply, to find a place where they would be left alone.

Members of one of the many Protestant separatist groups in post-Reformation England, they wanted to worship outside the Anglican Church because they felt it had not separated far enough from the Catholic Church. But the Pilgrims went further than most other sects; they wanted separation not only from the established Church but also from the secular culture that had what they saw as a corrupting influence on morals and behavior. Unable to find the religious freedom they sought in England, they acted on the text of Second Corinthians, "Come out from among them and be ye separate, saith the Lord," and withdrew to Leyden in Holland in 1608.

In Holland they were allowed to freely practice their faith but struggled for survival in this foreign, if tolerant, land. Still fearing that the purity of their religious ideas would be contaminated by the worldly culture, they sought a place where they might find not only freedom of worship but also freedom from the influence of non-believers. The Pilgrims, simply put, wanted to be alone with their god, to worship and live out their faith without outside influence. In this desire they stand in a long line of those who have sought refuge in the desert, on a mountain or on a remote island in an attempt to stay on the narrow road to salvation.

In 1620 some 35 Pilgrims from Holland embarked with about 65 other religious dissenters and 47 officers and crew on the *Mayflower*. They had obtained a grant to settle on a plantation in what is now New Jersey, then the far northern end of Virginia Colony. Blown off course during a nine week crossing, the little ship arrived off Cape Cod, Massachusetts, in December. Because they had missed Virginia, and had no title to lands at Plymouth, some 41 settlers before going ashore signed the Plymouth Compact, agreeing to obey any laws the community would create. The

Compact had no legal standing and the colony had no legal title to the land, but this early expression of their desire for and belief in self-government is one of the key documents in American history.

Determined to live strictly according to God's plan, the Pilgrims planted crops, built houses and spent a day in thanksgiving to God for the harvest. Their relations with the natives were helped immensely by an English-speaking Indian named Squanto, whom they saw as "a special instrument sent by God for their good beyond their expectation. He directed them how to set their corn, where to take fish, and to procure other commodities, and was also their pilot to bring them to unknown places for their profit, and never left them till he died."

In the end, having succeeded in overcoming the hardships of travel and the harsh reality of life in their new land, the Pilgrims succumbed to the danger they most feared – the influence of the culture around them. This time it was the effect of the larger and more powerful Puritan settlements based in Boston, which expanded rapidly until they absorbed Plymouth and its second- and third-generation Pilgrims by 1691. But the influence of these devout and courageous settlers has left an indelible mark on the collective conscience of America out of all proportion to their number.

The issue of these Pilgrim Tercentenary stamps in 1920, marking the 300th anniversary of their arrival, shows an idealized image of the *Mayflower* under full sail, the signing of the Compact and the landing at Cape Cod. Very unusually, the stamps did not bear the name of the United States and thus give no indication of the country that issued them.

Into the Wilderness

The Spanish continued to be the most active in exploring the New World throughout the 16th and early 17th centuries. In 1540 Francisco Coronado led an expedition through what is now Arizona and New Mexico searching for the legendary Seven Cities of Gold. The famous soldier is pictured on a stamp issued in 1940 on horseback accompanied by his captains and a priest to represent the Spanish empire moving forward physically and spiritually.

While New England and Virginia were being explored and claimed for Britain, another Englishman, Henry Hudson, sailed for the Dutch in 1609 and established the settlement of New Amsterdam on Manhattan Island. When the English assumed control of the Dutch possession in America in 1664, the settlement was renamed in honor

of the Duke of York. A stamp showing a characteristic Dutch windmill in the background, was issued to mark the 300th anniversary of the founding of New York City. The Walloons, who originated in Belgium and France, and the Huguenots, who were French Protestants, both settled on the Hudson River in the late 17th century. This two cent stamp marks the 300th anniversary of Walloon immigration and shows the landing at Fort Orange, the site of modern day Albany.

At about the same time, the French began to expand their presence along the St. Lawrence River. As early as 1534 Jacques Cartier began to trade for beaver pelts at Montreal and between 1603 and 1615 Samuel de Champlain, traveling mostly by canoe, explored and claimed much of the interior of North America for France. The one cent stamp, which shows Jacques Marquette on the Mississippi, is the first in a series of nine stamps commemorating the Trans-Mississippi Exposition held at Omaha, Nebraska, in 1898. Marquette was a Jesuit priest who founded several missions among the Indians. In 1675 he traveled with French explorer Louis Joliet as far as the present site of Chicago and the Mississippi River.

In 1701, Antoine de la Mothe Cadillac arrived at the river that flowed between Lake Huron and Lake Erie and at the narrowest point founded Detroit. This three cent stamp shows the modern skyline in the background and the first explorers coming ashore from their canoes.

In the 18th century, the English and French, traditional rivals for supremacy in Europe, now carried their rivalry into a race for trade, possessions and influence with the Indians in the New World. In April 1682 Jean-Baptiste de La Salle extended French claims in the New World to include the heart of the continent when he traveled down the Mississippi and claimed the land for France. They named it Louisiana in honor of Louis XIV, King of France. France now controlled both ends of the greatest river in North America and claimed all the lands in its watershed, an area that, although then unknown, stretched from the Appalachians to the Rocky Mountains.

UNITED STATES OF AMERICA

MARQUETTE ON THE MISSISSIPPI.

ONE — POSTAGE ONE CENT — ONE

U.S. POSTAGE — THREE CENTS

3¢

CORONADO AND HIS CAPTAINS

1540·CORONADO CUARTO CENTENNIAL·1940

POSTAGE 3¢ U.S.A.

300TH ANNIVERSARY OF NEW YORK CITY

U.S. POSTAGE

3¢

THE LANDING OF CADILLAC AT DETROIT·1701-1951

The same revolutionary beliefs
for which our forebears fought
are still at issue around the globe –
the belief that the rights of man
come not from the
generosity of the state,
but from the hand of God.

– John F. Kennedy

PART 3

CIVIL WARS

CIVIL WARS

The two most important wars in the history of the American nation were the Revolutionary War and the War Between the States. Both were, of course, civil wars in which neighbor fought against neighbor and families were divided; divided in 1776 over the question of remaining loyal to the King and then divided in 1860 over the question of remaining loyal to the Union. The alternative in both cases was embarking on a bold but dangerous bid for independence. The Revolution united the colonies in common cause against the British, but the bonds that were forged in 1776 had completely unraveled by 1860. The resolve that had held the colonies together to fight a war to become a nation was needed again to fight a war to preserve the Union.

The American Revolution was the result of the colonists' failure to secure recognition for themselves as Englishmen, with all the rights and privileges that entailed. Benjamin Franklin pointed out that taxation without representation was unconstitutional in England and therefore was also illegal in the English colonies. Unless the colonies were granted representation in Parliament, that Parliament could not tax them. This issue – the colonists' view of themselves as Englishmen who happened to live in America but were equal in every way to Englishmen living in England – was at the root of much of the language and action of the years between the end of the French and Indian War in 1763 and the confrontation at Lexington and Concord in 1775.

Although the move from protest to open rebellion was a long one, once the quest for representation had become a quest for independence, the struggle became a family feud, a civil war, between Englishmen. The loyalists were no less "American" than the patriots with whom they had been neighbors. Benjamin Franklin's eldest son remained in England as a loyal subject of the King throughout the war. At the end of the conflict, the loyalist refugees willing to leave behind everything they had worked so hard to acquire in the New World and move to British Canada alone numbered over 70,000. Many more returned to England or to other British colonies.

By 1860 another family struggle seemed inevitable. This time it had its origins in whether slavery was to be allowed in the western territories. Over this question,

11 southern states were determined to leave the Union to protect their way of life. Abraham Lincoln was declared elected as president on February 15, 1861. Before he formally took office on March 4, the South had seceded from the Union and declared its intention of forming a separate independent country. Congress and the President faced the question of how to respond. At stake was the future of the nation itself.

Lincoln put the issue succinctly in his Inaugural Address. After assuring the South that he had "no purpose, directly or indirectly, to interfere with the institution of slavery where it exists," he declared that he would not begin a war but warned that he would defend the Union if attacked. He made it clear that the decision was up to the South: "In your hands, my dissatisfied fellow-countrymen, and not in mine, is the momentous issue of civil war. The government will not assail you. You can have no conflict without being yourselves the aggressors. You have no oath registered in heaven to destroy the government, while I shall have the most solemn one to preserve, protect, and defend it ... we are not enemies, but friends. We must not be enemies. Though passion may have strained, it must not break our bonds of affection." This address was given on March 4, 1861. On April 12, South Carolina forces opened fire on Fort Sumter in Charleston Harbor. The bloodiest and most divisive war in the nation's history had begun. Although most of the citizens of the South fought for the Confederacy, four border states that permitted slavery – Kentucky, Maryland, Delaware and Missouri – decided to stay with the Union, and the western part of Virginia broke away and formed the new state of West Virginia.

It took over four years of bitter fighting before the war was over. Not only was the South beaten, it was exhausted, devastated and humiliated. Freed slaves were a daily reminder of the South's status as a conquered people. Having lost the war, the South was determined to deny the former slaves a place in society or a voice in government. It would take another 100 years, until the Civil Rights Movement of the 1960s, for the effects of the war to work themselves out and for all the nation's citizens to become equal in practice as well as principle. If freedom had been expensive to acquire, it proved even more expensive to preserve.

The American Revolution

When the Seven Years' War broke out in 1756, the English were determined not only to win the battle for supremacy in Europe but to win control of North America as well. In this war, for the first time, American colonists were called upon to form militia units for more than their own self-defense, and their participation in action all along the frontier helped to defeat the French and their Indian allies.

The colonies accomplished three essential things from their involvement in this European war on American soil: they raised their own militias and trained men to fight as a disciplined army; they acted together in a common cause rather than thinking and acting as 13 separate states; and they came to think of themselves as Americans clearly distinct from Englishmen. In short, they realized that their history, now comprising almost 150 years, in conjunction with their relative isolation from Europe, had given them more in common with each other than with England.

To help pay the enormous debts it incurred in the Seven Years' War, England had begun to raise money in America with the first Stamp Act of 1765. Despite protests by the colonists, the English maintained a permanent military force in the colonies to enforce their system of taxes and duties. By 1770 tensions had led to the Boston Massacre, in which British troops fired on protesters. In 1773 the events known as the Boston Tea Party made it clear that the colonists would not be easily intimidated. Hostility between the American colonies and the British had reached the point of armed conflict and the clash between Massachusetts militia and British regulars at Lexington and Concord in 1775 was truly a shot heard around the world.

Although the Revolution began as a protest over who had the power to tax and was fought and won on the battlefield, the American victory in the Revolutionary War defies explanation in strictly military and economic terms. Edmund Burke, in a speech to the House of Commons in London on September 3, 1783, urged reconciliation and recommended that the British government find a compromise that would avoid war with the American colonies.

Burke explained why Americans placed such a high value on liberty and why they would go to such lengths to secure it for themselves. The "fierce spirit of liberty is stronger in the English colonies probably than in any other people of the earth," he began. He proceeded to list the reasons: first, since Americans are "descendants of Englishmen," they are "devoted to liberty"; they are accustomed to a voice in their government and their representatives "inspire them with lofty sentiments"; and further, they are Protestants of a kind that is "averse to all implicit submission of mind and opinion." In areas of the world where slavery was common, as it was in the south, he added, those "who are free are by far the most proud and jealous of their freedom" and their haughtiness "combines with the spirit of freedom, fortifies it, and renders

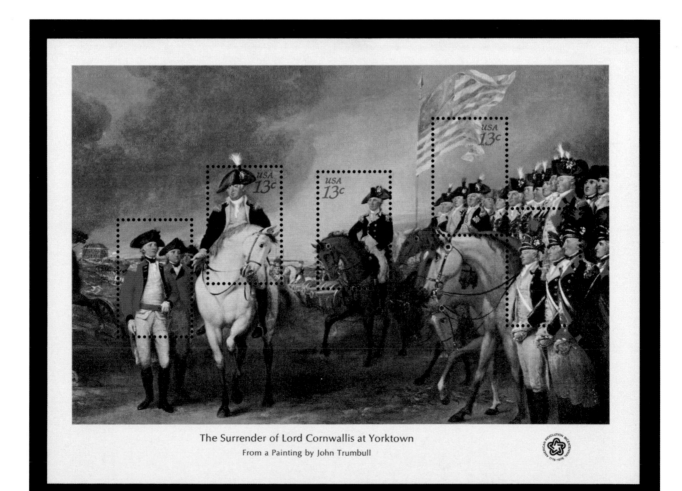

The Surrender of Lord Cornwallis at Yorktown

From a Painting by John Trumbull

it invincible." Americans also love the study of the law and this study makes them "snuff the approach of tyranny in every tainted breeze." In addition, Burke pointed out that 3,000 miles of ocean lay between England and America and that no efforts could "prevent the effect of this distance in weakening government."

For all these reasons Burke urged the House of Commons, in their need to raise tax revenues, to treat the colonists as Englishmen: "Let us get an American revenue as we have got an American empire. English privileges have made it all that it is; English privileges alone will make it all it can be." But Burke's words and good advice fell on deaf ears. Despite huge practical difficulties and conflicting interests, the colonies pulled together and, under George Washington's leadership, fought a difficult war that lasted eight years. In 1775 New England militiamen faced British troops at the Battle of Bunker Hill and ultimately forced the British to evacuate Boston. But Washington was defeated at the Battles of New York and Brooklyn Heights in 1776, and New York remained in British hands throughout the war. In 1777 the British were defeated at Princeton and at Brandywine and at the very important Battle of Saratoga. The American victory in this battle is widely credited with bringing the French into the war on the side of the Americans because it gave the French reason to believe that the Americans just might win.

But the end of the war was still a long way off. The British were victorious at Savannah in 1779, and at Charleston and Camden in 1780. General Cornwallis

hoped to secure the entire south, but Lafayette and Washington trapped his forces at Yorktown in 1781. His surrender convinced the British that they could not win the war, but official peace was not achieved until September 3, 1783. Popular legend has it that when Cornwallis surrendered the British military band played a popular tune called "The World Turned Upside Down." The story illustrates the significance of what had happened. Although two more years of struggle and negotiation remained until the last British troops left New York, the Americans had won the war against all odds. The world of rank and privilege in which Europe ruled supreme in the New World had indeed been turned upside down.

Throughout the war, Washington's forces had been greatly helped by experienced military leaders from Europe. Lafayette was the most famous but the three honored on the stamps shown on page 64, Pulaski, von Steuben and Kosciuszko, were all instrumental in the American victory.

When the war was over, Americans were quick to rebuild their ties to England and to resume their trade and commerce, both material and intellectual, with the nation from which they had sprung. King George III himself, who had failed to heed the urgings of his ministers to compromise with the colonies while there was still time to head off armed conflict, put best the reality of the situation when he received John Adams as the first American minister to the Court of St. James with these words: "I will be very frank with you. I was the last to consent to the separation; but the separation having been made, and having become inevitable, I have always said, as I say now, that I would be the first to meet the friendship of the United States as an independent power."

The experiment that is the United States had begun. The road ahead might not be easy, but there could be no nostalgia for a colonial past, no turning back the clock. Those who opposed independence either moved back to England with the retreating army, joined the great migration of loyalists who moved to British Canada, or accepted their fate and made the best of it. In 1812 America would again be at war with Britain to remove the last vestiges of their colonial heritage in international trade and commerce. By 1823 President Monroe would issue his famous doctrine declaring all of the New World, both North and South America, an American sphere of influence. Less than 40 years after independence, America was a power to be reckoned with.

Washington at Princeton 1777 by Peale
US Bicentennial 13c

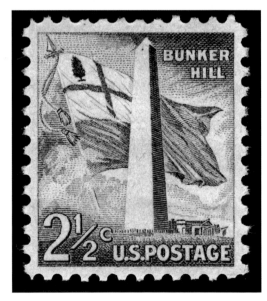

200TH ANNIVERSARY - THE BIRTH OF BETSY ROSS

UNITED STATES POSTAGE

3¢

ARRIVAL OF LAFAYETTE IN AMERICA · 1777

3¢ U.S. POSTAGE 3¢

Lexington & Concord 1775 by Sandham

US Bicentennial 10cents

Washington Crossing the Delaware

In this famous painting General George Washington is shown crossing the ice-choked Delaware River on Christmas day in 1776. His victory in the Battle of Trenton the next day provided a much-needed morale boost to the war effort. The painting, by Emanuel Leutze and Eastman Johnson, was done in Germany in 1851, more than 75 years after the actual battle. The people in the boat, representing the diversity of America's citizens, include a man with a Scottish bonnet, a Black American, men in western clothing, men wearing farmer's broad brimmed hats and a figure at the oar possibly meant to be a woman dressed in man's clothing. This picture remains one of the most famous images of the American Revolution.

The War Between the States

Less than a century after the colonies had achieved independence, the huge amount of land acquired through the Louisiana Purchase and the Mexican-American War was rapidly filling with a rough and ambitious people for whom Manifest Destiny was not a concept but an expression of their right to spread across the west and make of it what they could. Although by 1848 the United States reached from sea to sea, it was still a house divided against itself over the question of slavery, and the greatest test of its resolve to remain a nation was about to come.

When Missouri applied for admission as a state in 1819, half of the 22 states in the Union permitted slavery and half did not. In order to maintain a balance of slave states and free states in the senate, a compromise was reached: in 1821 Maine was admitted as a free state and Missouri as a slave state. This Missouri Compromise, as it was called, prohibited slavery in the remainder of the lands acquired in the Louisiana Purchase that were north of the southern boundary of Missouri. In 1857, however, the Supreme Court ruled that the Fifth Amendment to the Constitution made the Federal Government's prohibition of slavery in the territories unconstitutional because it deprived persons of their property – slaves were considered property – without due process of law. The language of the ruling also clearly stated that slaves were not citizens and thus had no rights before the courts: "It is too clear for dispute, that the enslaved African race were not intended to be included, and formed no part of the people who framed and adopted this declaration (of Independence)."

This decision reopened the debate on the expansion of slavery throughout the nation. In 1858, while running for a senate seat in Illinois, Abraham Lincoln had addressed the issue: "A house divided against itself cannot stand. I believe this government cannot endure, permanently half slave and half free. I do not

expect the Union to be dissolved – I do not expect the house to fall – but I do expect it will cease to be divided. It will become all one thing or all the other. Either the opponents of slavery will arrest the further spread of it, and place it where the public mind shall rest in the belief that it is in the course of ultimate extinction; or its advocates will push it forward, till it shall become alike lawful in all the States, old as well as new, North as well as South." Although he lost this bid for a senate seat, in 1860 the Republicans won the election and Lincoln was President. It was time to settle, once and for all, the question of slavery not only in the new territories but also in the nation itself.

From the point of view of the South, what became the bloodiest war in American history was ultimately about the same issue as the Revolution – the right of a free people to disobey the laws of their government and form a new nation if they felt that the govern-

ment was not acting in their best interest. But the North was insistent that the Union, once entered into, was permanent and insoluble and that the states were and always would be subordinate to the Federal Government.

Although it provides an easily grasped and emotionally powerful symbol, the existence of slavery in the southern states was not the only cause of the war. The North and South had developed very differently since 1776. The issue of taxes on imported goods was a constant thorn to both sides. The North wanted high tariffs to protect its industrial base, but the South wanted low tariffs to make imports cheaper. The North was primarily an urban, western-facing industrial power and the destination for most immigrants from Europe. The South's economy was agrarian; its leaders were gentlemen farmers whose life on huge plantations worked by slaves had changed little since the end of the 18th century.

Slavery certainly was seen as a moral evil throughout the north, but the war was fought to preserve the Union and not to free the slaves. Lincoln himself professed his willingness to preserve the Union at any cost: "My paramount object in this struggle is to save the Union, and is not either to save or to destroy slavery. If I could save the Union without freeing any slave I would do it, and if I could save it by freeing all the slaves I would do it; and if I could save it by freeing some and leaving others alone, I would also do that. What I do about slavery, and the colored race, I do because I believe it helps to save the Union; and what I forbear, I forbear because I do not believe it would help to save the Union."

As with any civil war, this one divided friends and families as well as states. Mary Todd, the president's wife, had a sister who was married to a Confederate general. When he was killed at the Battle of Chickamauga, the sister came north and moved into the White House to live with the President's family. Robert E. Lee, the most able commander of the war and a man whose integrity was unquestioned by either side, was offered command of the Union Army by Lincoln as well as command of the Army of Northern Virginia. Forced to choose between his country and his state, Lee stood by his decision to fight for Virginia. At the end of the war, despite all the death and devastation, he remained firm: "We could have pursued no other course without dishonor. And sad as the results have been, if it had all to be done over again, we should be compelled to act in precisely the same manner." It was honor, then, that was at stake – the right of the people of the South to determine their own destiny.

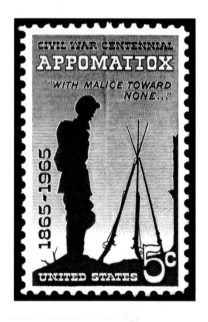

Whatever the causes, the result was dreadful in the extreme; some 620,000 men are estimated to have died in battle or from disease. From the first shot at Fort Sumter to Lee's surrender at Appomattox more than four years later, the South fought valiantly, but the superior manpower and supplies of the North made defeat inevitable. The longer the conflict lasted, the lower were the South's chances of winning this war of attrition fought on its own soil. By the end the South was exhausted, humiliated and in ruins. The plantation economy was devastated, the slaves were free and the Union Army was in command. The North had sacrificed men and materials, but its mighty economy had prospered during the war and the United States was now one of the world's great industrial powers.

Abraham Lincoln

In this portrait, the stress and toll that Lincoln's years in office had taken on the man is apparent. When the brutal Civil War was at last over, Lincoln planned to heal the wounds by bringing the South back into the Union as quickly as possible. His assassination, however, ended hopes for a quick reconciliation. Georgia was the last of the Confederate States to be readmitted to the Union in 1870 and military intervention in the south would last until 1877. The Civil War was the first major event in American history to be captured in photographs that give us an unparalleled look at what still remains the most crucial war in American history. This stamp, issued on February 12, 1923, shows the Lincoln Memorial in Washington, D. C. One of the most famous buildings in the world, it is visited by millions of people from around the world each year. Inside the memorial are inscribed the words from his Second Inaugural Address, "with malice toward none; with charity for all; with firmness in the right, as God gives us to see the right, let us strive

on to finish the work we are in; to bind up the nation's wounds." Second only to George Washington, Abraham Lincoln retains his place as one of the truly great presidents and his hold on the popular imagination as a man of the people who rose to greatness in dangerous times.

Battle of Gettysburg

Gettysburg was one of the most critical battles of the War Between the States. General Robert E. Lee had crossed the Potomac River and marched into Pennsylvania in June 1863; now Philadelphia, Baltimore and Washington were under threat of attack. From the beginning of the war, the South had hoped to capture Washington and force the Union to negotiate a settlement and recognize its independence. The Union and Confederate forces met in the small town of Gettysburg on July 1, 1863. The Confederate forces attacked the well-fortified Union positions again and again. In three days of bitter fighting in which cannon and rifle fire decimated the troops, over 50,000 men were killed before Lee retreated back into Virginia. The tide of war had turned. The South had failed in its attempt to carry the battle into the North and would never regain the initiative. But years of deadly struggle remained. On November 19th Lincoln traveled to the battlefield to dedicate a military cemetery to hold the dead. His remarks, delivered

in only a little over two minutes, express the obligation we have to those who have paid the ultimate price for our freedom: "We here highly resolve that these dead shall not have died in vain ... that this government of the people, by the people, for the people, shall not perish from the earth." This stamp was issued on July 1, 1963.

The fulfillment of our manifest
destiny to overspread the continent
allotted by Providence for the free
development of our yearly
multiplying millions.

– John O'Sullivan

MANIFEST DESTINY

MANIFEST DESTINY

The entire American experience, from the moment the first settlers boarded ships in England and Europe to sail west across the Atlantic, might be epitomized by the famous maxim attributed to editor Horace Greeley, "Go west, young man, and grow up with the country."

The Appalachian Mountains were the first natural and political barrier that would slow, but not prevent, America's inexorable drive to open up the west. By the end of the Revolutionary War the country had gained possession of lands as far west as the Mississippi River. In 1803, with the Louisiana Purchase, the boundary moved still farther west to the Rocky Mountains, and with the 1848 treaty ending the Mexican-American War the western boundary of the nation reached the Pacific Ocean.

All this new land, acquired in just 65 years between 1783 and 1848, brought with it the need to deal with the unresolved question of slavery. Although politicians reassured the South that the Federal Government had no intention – and indeed no power – to interfere with slavery where it already existed, the extension of slavery into the new territories and states was another matter altogether, a matter destined to be settled not by words but by war.

At the end of the War Between the States, thousands of displaced men from both armies, southerners uprooted by the devastation of war and immigrants seeking opportunity and adventure, poured west across the Mississippi. The Homestead Act of 1862 granted clear title to up to 160 acres of public land absolutely free to anyone who had not fought against the Union and who would settle the land and remain on it for five years. The transcontinental railway, completed in 1869, provided a way west for the settlers and a way east for the products of their mines, ranches and farms.

The legendary lawless west, immortalized in the symbol of the American cowboy, stems from the short period between 1865 and 1885 when the arrival of the settlers often preceded the establishment of effective government. By 1893, when the World's Columbian Exposition in Chicago celebrated the 400th anniversary of Columbus's arrival in America, the nation could show millions of visitors that in little more than 100 years it had not only stretched across the continent but also had become one of the greatest industrial and military powers in the world. The west was largely tamed and settled, and its great adventures were now relived in traveling "wild west" shows with their dramatic and often fanciful recreation of a vanished world. Yet so strong was the lure of the west, with its emphasis on courage, independence and self-reliance, that these shows found huge audiences in the United States, England and Europe. Later, books, music, movies – and ultimately television – all featured cowboy heroes as the battle for the west became a key feature of 20th-century American mythology.

By 1900, with the frontier officially closed, it remained for America in the new century to forge its vast and divergent possessions and populations into a single nation. Obliged, usually against its will, to take center stage in world affairs, and yet profoundly uninterested in the world outside its borders, the nation seemed to hover uneasily between dreams of influence and isolation.

Northwest of the River Ohio

In 1783 the United States, having just fought to escape from colonial status itself, found it had "colonies" of its own – lands acquired at the end of the Revolutionary War that were not part of the original 13 colonies. Once the individual states had ceded their western land claims to the Federal Government, Congress had to administer these territories until they acquired sufficient population to apply for statehood and full participation in the Union.

In 1787 Congress passed the Northwest Ordinance to govern the territories that lay between the Appalachian Mountains and the Mississippi River and were "northwest of the River Ohio." This area became collectively known as the Northwest Territory. This huge expanse of land was later split into smaller territories, which were divided into two categories: an "organized" territory had formed its own local government; and an "unorganized" territory was administered directly by Congress without any local assembly.

The Ordinance of 1787 provided that Congress would appoint a governor, secretary and three judges who were responsible for the territory until a general assembly could be formed. A territory had to be "organized" before it could be considered for admission as a state. To become organized, the population had to reach "five thousand free male inhabitants" who were then entitled to elect a general assembly

on the basis of one representative "for every five hundred free male inhabitants."

Article 3 of the Ordinance stipulated: "The utmost good faith shall always be observed towards the Indians; their lands and property shall never be taken from them without their consent." Article 6 provided that there should be "neither slavery nor involuntary servitude in the said territory, otherwise than in the punishment of crimes" but that an escaped slave must be captured and "conveyed to the person claiming his or her labor or service."

Finally, the Ordinance stated that when a territory's population reached 60,000 "free inhabitants" it could be admitted to the Union as a new state "on an equal footing with the original States in all respects whatever" and be "at liberty to form a permanent constitution and State government." This system provided the basic structure for future territorial government and was used to administer territories and admit states to the Union as the nation acquired more land and expanded westward. Ohio, the key territory in the Northwest frontier, was admitted as a state in 1803.

The Northwest, Oregon, Kansas, Minnesota, Washington and Nebraska Territories are commemorated on these stamps. The Minnesota stamp shows the famous Red River ox cart, while the Kansas stamp features an image of the wagons that carried the settlers westward.

From Sea to Shining Sea

While English settlers were establishing colonies along the Atlantic coast, French explorers and traders followed the great water route from Québec up the St. Lawrence River, through the Great Lakes and down the Mississippi River to New Orleans and claimed the entire interior of the continent for France. By 1748 both the French and English were moving into the rich lands of the Ohio Valley, and conflict became inevitable.

The future of the heart of North America was settled by the Seven Years' War between Britain and France. British victory created a demand among American colonists for access to the rich lands west of the Appalachians. The British government refused to open the land to settlement because of its treaties with the Indians and its desire to keep the colonies from becoming too large and thinly settled to be effectively defended or governed. With or without official permission, however, a trickle of settlers began to travel over the mountains. In 1775, even as the

Revolution was beginning, Daniel Boone's Wilderness Road led the first groups of settlers into what would become Kentucky. After the Revolution, the trickle would become a flood.

By 1803 four new states had joined the Union and settlers were rapidly moving toward the Mississippi River, then the western frontier. President Thomas Jefferson, fearing that Napoleon would send troops to Louisiana and establish a French empire in America, sent a delegation to France with instructions to offer Napoleon $10 million for New Orleans and Florida or $7.5 million for New Orleans alone. Either purchase would guarantee America control of the mouth of the Mississippi River and ensure its ability to protect its western border. Desperate to pay for his wars in Europe, Napoleon offered to sell not just New Orleans but all of Louisiana Territory to Robert Livingston, the head of the American delegation, for $15 million.

At the stroke of a pen, the United States had doubled in size and now stretched from the Atlantic Ocean to the Rocky Mountains across millions of acres of unexplored wilderness. Jefferson authorized an expedition to explore the new lands and find out just what it was that the United States had bought. In May 1804 Meriwether Lewis and William Clark led the famous Lewis and Clark expedition west from St. Louis along the Missouri River. In November 1805 they found the Columbia River and saw the Pacific Ocean. It was the first time Americans had caught a glimpse of what lay at the end of the frontier.

Remember the Alamo

Having reached the shores of the Pacific, the American settlers, traders and explorers who followed in the footsteps of Lewis and Clark flowed south through the invisible and mostly undefined border with Mexico's northern possessions. For some time Americans had been moving into Texas and by the 1830s outnumbered the Mexican settlers. Afraid of losing control of the lands north of the Rio Grande River, Mexico imposed restrictions on further American immigration into Texas and abolished slavery, a move guaranteed to antagonize the American settlers, who came largely from the slave-holding south.

In 1835, with the Mexican government preoccupied with political revolt at home, American settlers in Texas demanded recognition of their rights and then full independence from Mexico. The Mexican government sent General Santa Anna and 6,000 men to quell the rebellion and secure the area. The Americans made a stand against a much larger Mexican force at a small mission station called the Alamo. Santa Anna captured the Alamo and mercilessly executed all those who had been taken prisoner. The slaughter outraged the settlers, and "Remember the Alamo!" became their battle cry. When Santa Anna was captured after the Battle of Jacinto in 1836, he was forced to sign a document recognizing Texas's independence. The United States remained neutral in this conflict and Texas became an independent republic.

When the United States finally agreed to admit Texas to the Union in 1845, conflict over land ownership, the status of Texas, and American claims in California led to war between the United States and Mexico in 1846. Mexico could not hold these sparsely settled lands so remote from Mexico City, and at the end of the war, in 1848, was forced to cede a huge expanse of land, which included what are now California, New Mexico, Arizona, Nevada, Utah and Colorado. The end of the war and the acquisition of the southwest came just as tens of thousands of Americans poured west in the California Gold Rush. The final boundary between Mexico and the United States was established in 1853 when James Gadsden was sent to Mexico to acquire a route for a southern transcontinental railway to California. He purchased about 30,000 square miles of territory for $10 million along the southern border of what are currently New Mexico and Arizona.

In 1846 the Oregon Settlement between Britain and the United States had settled the boundary between Canada and the United States at the 49th parallel. America now stretched across the continent, from sea to shining sea. Her "manifest destiny" had become a reality.

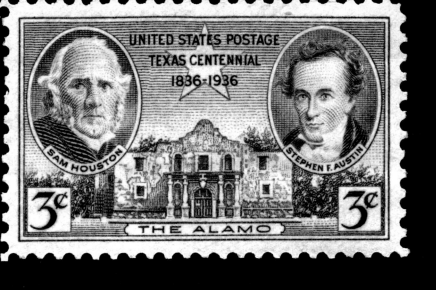

UNITED STATES POSTAGE
TEXAS CENTENNIAL
1836-1936

SAM HOUSTON

STEPHEN F. AUSTIN

3¢

3¢

THE ALAMO

STEPHEN WATTS
KEARNY
EXPEDITION

US POSTAGE

3¢

1846 ENTRY INTO SANTA FE 1946

CALIFORNIA   ARIZONA   NEW MEXICO

1853
GADSDEN
PURCHASE

MEXICO

RIO GRANDE

TEXAS

3¢   U.S. POSTAGE

The California Gold Rush

California had become part of the United States at the end of the Mexican-American War in 1848. The territory was remote from the settled East and accessible only by ships sailing around Cape Horn or the long and difficult overland routes. But the difficulties of travel were ignored as Americans rushed west after the discovery of gold at Sutter's Mill in 1848. For a brief period gold nuggets of amazing purity could be found in the rivers and streams. The heavy yellow metal settled to the bottom of the miner's pan as he sifted through the sand and gravel. More than 350,000 people came west in search of gold between 1848 and 1860. Few grew rich but most remained in the west and California had sufficient population to qualify for statehood by 1850. An estimated $250,000,000 of gold was found in the twenty years from 1849 to 1869. But costs soared in the mining camps with a single egg costing as much as $3, and violence and hardship were a way of life. Throughout the west and later in Alaska the search for gold, silver and other minerals would continue throughout the century and the

dream of making the next big strike would be enough to make men endure incredible hardship and danger. California, the golden land of opportunity and beauty, continues to attract Americans from across the nation and is today the most populous state in the Union. This stamp was issued on January 24, 1948.

The Homestead Act

After the end of the Civil War the west exerted a pull like a magnet on the imagination of Americans and immigrants from every nation. The transcontinental railroad made it easier to travel but when the settlers arrived and began to farm the land, hardship awaited on a scale unimaginable today. To induce people to settle the western lands, Congress passed the Homestead Act and it was signed by President Lincoln on May 20, 1862. The Act offered 160 acres of land free to any person who had not fought against the United States so long as that person remained on the land for a period of five years, improved it and built a dwelling measuring at least 12 x 14 feet. For those with money, land was available in unlimited amounts at $1.25 an acre. The image on the stamp, a woman in the doorway of her sod hut talking to her husband who is busy conquering unbroken wilderness with a shovel, suggests a world of hardship and toil as well as opportunity. But these hardy people endured and they triumphed. The west was won, and by the end of the 19th century prosperous farmers and their wives could,

like those in this 1890 photograph, dressed in their Sunday best pose on the farm machinery that lessened some of the backbreaking work. The Homestead Act was not repealed until 1976 (Alaska was granted a 10-year extension) by which time more than 270 million acres had been claimed. This stamp was issued on May 20, 1962.

Trans-Mississippi Exposition 1898

The Trans-Mississippi Exposition, held in Omaha, Nebraska, in 1898, covered more than 100 city blocks and featured over 4,000 exhibits. One of the most popular exhibits was the huge Indian Congress with 28 tribes displaying their native customs. August 31 was designated as "Cody Day" in honor of Buffalo Bill Cody, who brought his famous Wild West Show back to the city where it had been founded.

A re-enactment of the explosion of the battleship *Maine* in Havana Harbor was held daily to generate support for the Spanish-American war then being fought. Over two and a half million people visited the fair, and both President William McKinley and William Jennings Bryan addressed large crowds. The celebration of the settlement of the west was a fitting theme for the close of the 19th century. Each stamp in this series features a scene connected with the settlement and development of the lands west of the Mississippi River.

The 1¢ stamp shows the Jesuit missionary Jacques Marquette, one of the first Europeans to explore the Mississippi River.

The 2¢ stamp, showing the grand scale of farming on the limitless prairie, is based on a picture showing 61 horses and machinery working a section of land.

The 4¢ stamp features an Indian hunting buffalo with a bow and arrow before the near-extinction of these animals destroyed the way of life of many Native Americans.

The 5¢ stamp commemorates the moment when explorer John Charles Fremont raised the American flag on one of the tallest peaks in the Rocky Mountains.

The 8¢ stamp shows military troops protecting a wagon train of settlers from Indian attack as the westward push of settlement forced the Indians from their land.

The 10¢ stamp depicts the hardship of early pioneer life; the death or sickness of an animal could leave an emigrating family stranded on the prairie.

The 50¢ stamp, which features a mining prospector leading his mules as he searches for gold, is based on a drawing by Frederick Remington.

The $1.00 stamp, often considered the most beautiful American stamp ever issued, shows western cattle in a storm but was actually based on a painting of cattle in the Scottish Highlands.

The $2.00 stamp is taken from an engraving of the Eads Bridge, the first bridge to span the Mississippi at St. Louis and thus physically and symbolically link the American east and west.

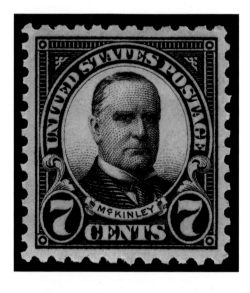

Pan-American Exposition 1901

The first American commemorative stamps of the 20th century were issued to celebrate the 1901 Pan-American Exposition held in Buffalo, New York. The Trans-Mississippi issue of 1898 had looked back at the hardship, danger and adventure of settling the west; this issue, created only three years later, looked resolutely to the future. Half of the stamps have "FAST" in their caption, an indication of the energy that characterized the nation at the beginning of the 20th century.

The 1¢ stamp features the *City of Alpena*, a steamer that provided regular passenger and freight service on the Great Lakes. The 2¢ stamp shows the New York Central Railroad's *Empire State Express* flying along near its top speed of 100 miles per hour.

The 4¢ stamp pictures an early electric automobile used by the Baltimore & Ohio Railroad to deliver passengers to their destinations within Washington, D.C. In 1901 electric cars were considered more reliable than gasoline-powered vehicles.

The 5¢ stamp features the Bridge at Niagara Falls, then the longest single-span bridge in the world. It was a natural subject for this series, since Buffalo, the site of the exposition, is the nearest large American city to the falls and electricity from Niagara Falls illuminated the city and the exposition.

The 8¢ stamp shows the canal and locks at Sault Ste. Marie which linked Lake Superior to the rest of the Great Lakes at the Michigan-Ontario border. The locks allowed ships to bring ore south to the great iron and steel factories of the Midwest during America's turn-of-the-century industrial expansion. The canal was an engineering marvel in an era of worldwide canal-building activity, which included the construction of the Panama and Suez canals.

The 10¢ stamp shows the American ship *St. Paul*, representing the age of the luxury liner crossing the Atlantic in speed and comfort. The *St. Paul* was the first commercial ship to be taken over by the government and used in the Spanish-American War and so was a fitting symbol of commerce and patriotism at the time.

The Pan-American Exhibition is mostly remembered today as the place where President William McKinley was assassinated. At his death Theodore Roosevelt became president.

Expansion Overseas

As the 19th century drew to a close the country was widening its sphere of influence beyond the boundaries of the continental United States. Americans, opposed since George Washington to involvement in European political entanglements and empires, had until now relied on two great oceans for protection against foreign armies and foreign influence. The energy and drive that characterized the nation had been absorbed in conquering and settling the west and producing wealth and industry in abundance. Still viewing itself as the refuge for the world's poor and oppressed, most Americans had no ambition for overseas expansion and the acquisition of empire.

Nevertheless, America's overseas trade across the Pacific had begun to draw the nation yet further west as early as 1854, when a naval force commanded by Matthew Perry forced Japan to abandon its own policy of isolation and begin trading with the United States. By the end of the Civil War, the United States had one of the strongest industrial economies in the world and could no longer avoid involvement in international trade and political agreements. In 1867 the United States purchased Alaska from Russia and annexed Midway Island to provide a refueling station for the Pacific navy. A naval base was established at Samoa in 1878 and at Pearl Harbor in Hawaii by 1887. In 1898 the Hawaiian Islands were formally annexed by the United States, largely to protect them from domination by the Japanese.

But it was events in Cuba, only 90 miles from Florida, which provided the catalyst for American expansion overseas. The great Spanish Empire, begun 400 years previously in 1492, had flourished and then slowly withered away. By 1895 only Cuba, the Philippines and Puerto Rico remained under Spanish control. When Cuban rebels tried to overthrow Spanish rule and gain independence, expansionist elements in the United States pushed for American intervention. In response to American pressure, the Spanish government granted concessions to the rebels but when the American battleship *Maine* exploded and sank in Havana harbor, the United States declared war on Spain.

The Spanish fleets stationed in Cuba and the Philippines were quickly sunk. Cuba was occupied and granted limited independence under strong American influence. The United States' attempt to rule the Philippines, however, was met with stiff resistance and a long guerrilla war.

Encouraged by President Theodore Roosevelt, who had risen to fame at the head of the Rough Riders (volunteer cavalry that fought in Cuba), rebel groups in Panama broke away from Colombia. They granted American firms the right to build a canal across the isthmus linking the Atlantic and Pacific Oceans in fulfillment of a centuries-old dream of a water route to the east.

Although each step toward overseas expansion, from the purchase of Alaska to the Spanish-American War to the

recognition of Panama, had been highly controversial and bitterly opposed by many in Congress, by the dawn of the 20th century an American overseas empire had become a reality.

These four stamps celebrate the expansion of the United States. Puerto Rico became an American colony in 1898 at the end of the Spanish-American War. In 1917 American citizenship was granted to island residents and in 1952 the Commonwealth of Puerto Rico was proclaimed. The Virgin Islands, a group of 68 small islands, mostly uninhabited, were bought from Denmark in 1917 to serve as a naval base that would help protect the Panama Canal. Today the islands' residents are American citizens. Alaska was acquired from Russia in 1867 for $7.2 million. Many in Congress opposed the purchase. However, in 1896 gold was discovered in the Klondike and a gold rush drew thousands north. Alaska, the largest but the most sparsely populated state, joined the Union in 1959 as the 49th state.

Hawaii is a group of some 100 islands in the Pacific, 2,400 miles from California. American whalers, traders and missionaries dominated the islands. When Queen Liliuokalani opposed American political and business domination, she was deposed in a bloodless revolution, and in 1893 the Republic of Hawaii was proclaimed. The United States annexed Hawaii in 1898 and it became the 50th state in 1959.

I will build a motor car for the great

multitude . . . it will be so low in

price that no man making a good

salary will be unable to own one –

and enjoy with his family the

blessings of hours of pleasure

in God's great open spaces.

– Henry Ford

PART 5

TRANSPORTATION AND COMMUNICATION

TRANSPORTATION AND COMMUNICATION

The continental United States, stretching from the Atlantic to the Pacific Ocean and from Canada to Mexico, is one of the largest nations in the world. Even today a trip across the continent can take a week. When the first Europeans reached North America, the land must have seemed to go on forever. To people familiar with European towns and cities so small that a wall could be built around them, life on the edge of a vast, unknown wilderness must have been daunting but at the same time wonderfully liberating.

One aspect of the American character that would later be summed up in the phrase "Go West Young Man" was the restlessness that seemed to compel each generation of Americans to move farther west in search of new lands, greater opportunity and personal freedom. The western frontier began on the beaches of the Atlantic Ocean as the first settlers stepped foot on these shores. Although the immediate geographical challenges changed, the idea of moving west in search of a better life virtually defined the American dream for almost three centuries.

The *Mayflower*'s long and dangerous journey across the Atlantic took nine weeks, about the same time as Columbus's first voyage more than a century before. Although the first settlers could not know it then, even more unimaginable distances awaited them. The distance between what would one day be the cities of Boston and Los Angeles was almost as great as the distance they had just sailed from England.

But the vast fertile lands that stretched across the interior of the American continent were virtually inaccessible in an age when good roads were practically nonexistent and overland travel was a matter of weeks and months, not days. Forests, rivers, mountains and deserts presented seemingly insurmountable obstacles to settlement but each would, in turn, be overcome with advances in river transport, road building, trains and automobiles. Transportation was a major challenge to the new nation. Its availability would determine where settlement occurred and how successful it would be.

The first highways into the interior were the great rivers that flow across the continent. The Mississippi and Missouri Rivers were critical to early settlement and control of the interior. It was the need to control the mouth of the Mississippi that prompted Thomas Jefferson to make the Louisiana Purchase in 1803. The immense land the nation acquired was a bonus; what Jefferson wanted was control of the river that formed the western boundary of the nation. By the 1820s steamboats could travel upstream against the current carrying heavy loads and river traffic entered its golden age. The Erie Canal in New York was one of the engineering wonders of the world for its time and one of the most successful financial enterprises in the young nation. Only with the coming of the railroad would rivers and canals lose their pre-eminence in American transportation.

The need to establish methods of travel over the land was matched by the need to establish a reliable communication system. The first postal system was established in the colonies as early as 1673 but communication was slow and sporadic. It was not until the railroad tracks and telegraph poles marched – often side-by-side as the telegraph followed the railroad right-of-way – into every corner of the nation between 1870 and 1900 that the speed and reliability of communication would begin to approach modern standards.

But the real advance in transportation that came to define America in the 20th century and imprint itself on the American character itself was the automobile. Freed at last from the schedules and predetermined routes of trains, ships, buses and airplanes, we had the liberty to go where we wished and when we wished. In 1900 the average person might not travel more than a few miles a day to go from home to work or shopping or visiting friends. Cities were compact because people had to walk from place to place. But automobiles gave rise to suburbs and the two-car families that commonly drive 100 miles in a day.

Realizing man's age-old dream of flight was another, even greater, triumph of American ingenuity and manufacturing skill. Less than 25 years after the Wright brothers' first flight in 1903, which lasted 12 seconds and covered 120 feet, Charles Lindbergh would fly 3,600 miles non-stop across the Atlantic in little more than 33 hours. And only 42 years after that, in 1969, Neil Armstrong would put an American flag on the moon while the world watched. The incredible advances in transportation had made it possible for us to travel in comfort at unprecedented speeds. And when we couldn't go personally, advances in communication allowed us to turn on the television and see things happening in real time. History had come into the living room. We did indeed live in a global village.

River Roads

Although much of the east coast of the United States was served by well-marked dirt roads by the middle of the 18th century, these roads frequently became impassable after rain or snow and were totally inadequate for shipping heavy loads year round on a regular schedule. Early settlers moving west relied instead on rivers, especially the Hudson, the Ohio, the Mississippi and the Missouri, as the principal highways into the interior.

Sails had driven ocean-going ships for thousands of years and brought the colonists or their ancestors to these shores, but away from the coasts sailing was confined to very large bodies of water like the Great Lakes, where dependable winds, deep water and long distances made the use of sailing ships practical. On rivers, barges, pushed along by poles jammed into muddy

riverbeds, carried much of the freight until wood-burning, shallow-draft steamboats revolutionized travel. Especially on the Mississippi and the Missouri, steamboats made it possible to travel upriver against the current and to carry heavy loads on a reliable schedule.

With rivers and lakes the only economical highway on which to transport goods and people, the idea of linking these natural water highways together with a system of locks and canals to create a water route into the heart of the continent had irresistible appeal. The greatest of the American canal-building ventures was the famous Erie Canal, which linked the Hudson River with Lake Erie when it was completed in 1825.

The Erie Canal opened the lands of western New York and the Ohio Valley to settlement and provided access to New York markets for the produce of the frontier. Before the canal was built, it cost about $100 to transport a ton of wheat by wagon from the Genesee Valley to Albany, New York, and the trip took 20 days. Once in Albany the wheat would be loaded onto a boat for the trip down the Hudson to New York City. Using the canal, the cost dropped to only $5 to ship a ton of wheat all the way to New York. By 1845 the canal was handling a million tons of people, crops and manufactured goods a year. The produce of the west could finally reach world markets and the manufactured goods of the east could reach the settlers in the interior. Although its role was dramatically reduced with the coming of the railway, the Erie Canal played no small part in the opening of the Northwest Territory and in the rise of New York as the largest and most important city in America.

In 1855 the canal at Sault Ste. Marie on the Michigan-Ontario border linked Lake Superior to the rest of the Great Lakes and the world beyond. The completion of the 2,342-mile St. Lawrence Seaway in 1959 fulfilled the dream that ocean-going vessels could sail deep into the continent, through the Seaway and the Great Lakes to Chicago as well as to the northwest reaches of Lake Superior.

Canal building to link major waterways was undertaken around the world in the 19th century, perhaps most notably at Suez in Egypt and in Panama. The Panama Canal, a combination of canals and locks linking natural and man-made lakes, eliminated a long, hazardous journey around South America for ships sailing from east coast ports to California and China. The Suez Canal eliminated the trip around Africa from Europe to the East. But the little Erie Canal remains a fitting symbol of the ingenuity and resourcefulness of the American dream.

From Sail to Steam

The first large cities and towns in the original colonies were established on the shores of good natural harbors. Boston, New York, Philadelphia and Baltimore all became major ocean ports. Shipbuilding, one of the first industries in the New World, is celebrated on the three cent Popham Colony stamp. Popham, the first English colony in the New World, was founded in 1607 and lasted for a little over a year during which time the colonists built the little ship *Virginia* shown on this stamp.

Sailing ships brought the early settlers to America and linked the country with Europe and the Orient. Rivers and canals became the first American highways into the interior and, until the coming of the railroad, dominated the inland movement of goods and passenger traffic.

The history of the steamboat in America goes all the way back to 1787 when John Fitch made a successful trial run on the Delaware River, but it was Robert Fulton who made the first commercially successful steamboat. In 1807 his *Clermont*, moving about five miles an hour, traveled from New York City to Albany, New York, a distance of 150 miles in 32 hours. Fulton's *Clermont* and Hudson's ship *Half Moon* are shown on the two cent stamp issued in 1909 to mark the discovery of the great river and the importance of the steamboat. By 1814 regular steamboat service by paddle wheeler was available between New Orleans and Natchez, Mississippi, at eight miles an hour downstream and three miles an hour upstream.

Water transportation, particularly shipping on the Great Lakes, was of paramount importance to the settlement of the West. In 1818 the first steamship on Lake Erie, the *Walk-in-the-Water*, was put into service. A report published in 1836 recalls the impact of the new invention: "The novelty of the sight, as she made her first trip through the lake, excited a great degree of interest and curiosity among the people who lived upon the shores, especially among the native Indians, who were ignorant of the power and application of steam. They stood gazing with astonishment to see such 'a thing of life' moving through the water without the aid of oars or sail."

In 1835 there were 34 steamboats operating on Lake Erie alone. "Multitudes of highly respectable families who are emigrating to the West prefer to take a deck passage rather than to pay the price of a cabin." The fee for steerage from Buffalo to Detroit was $3, while cabin passage cost $8.

In 1819 the *Savannah*, shown on the three cent stamp with sails furled, used a steam-driven paddle wheel to supplement its sails and completed the ocean voyage from Savannah, Georgia, to Liverpool, England, in 29 days. The first completely steam-powered ocean crossing was made in 1839, and the *Great Britain*, the first iron-hulled, propeller-driven ship, was launched in 1843.

From Shore to Shore

The great increase in bridge building in the United States coincided with improvements in the production and quality of iron and steel in the last half of the 19th century. The railway bridge dominated construction until the 1920s, when the huge increase in car and truck traffic created a demand for bridges to link highways across the nation.

The Eads Bridge across the Mississippi River secured St. Louis its position as the Gateway to the West and was considered an engineering triumph when it opened in 1874. The 6,442-foot bridge has three spans that rest on stone pillars anchored to the bedrock below the river and was the first major bridge to use steel and exclusively cantilevered support methods.

The Verrazano-Narrows Bridge connecting Brooklyn with Staten Island is named after Giovanni da Verrazano. In 1524 he was the first European sailor to explore New York Harbor. This suspension bridge, opened in 1964, measures 4,260 feet between its two giant towers and supports a double-decked roadway. The bridge is so huge that seasonal expansion of the cables because of heat causes it to be 12 feet lower in summer than in winter.

The Mackinac Straits Bridge, another record-breaking suspension bridge, was the outcome of a long history of attempts to link the two peninsulas that comprise the state of Michigan. In 1923 Michigan established a regular ferry service across the strait but the traffic was soon so heavy that a bridge was clearly needed. But the expense was too great for a nation coping with a depression and then a war. Finally the 8,614-foot long bridge opened to traffic on November 1, 1954.

The Peace Bridge, which crosses from Buffalo, New York, to Fort Erie, Ontario, reflects the importance of Canadian-American trade. Its name acknowledges the peaceful relations between the United States and Canada, which share the longest undefended border in the world. As early as 1848 a cable was strung across the Niagara River so that a basket could be pulled from side to side. The basket could carry 125 passengers a day at a cost of $1.00 each for a return trip. A railway bridge was built spanning the river in 1873 and the Peace Bridge, designed for pedestrian and automobile traffic, opened in 1927. The bridge consists of five arched spans and is 5,800 feet long. Until 1992 the Peace Bridge was the busiest border crossing between the two countries.

Bridges have been so significant in the development of the United States that the stamp issued in 1952 honoring the centennial of engineering features a bridge to symbolize the contribution that engineering has made to the nation.

Ribbons of Steel

Horses, stagecoaches, wagon trains, buckboards and ox carts all carried people and goods across the country for two centuries after the landing of the *Mayflower*. The change occasioned by the railroad in the shipment of people and goods was nothing short of revolutionary. For the first time in history people could travel faster than a horse could run, and do it for hours without stopping. Especially in America, with its vast distances, the railway bound the nation together with a ribbon of steel and changed the way we thought about distance and travel.

The precursors of today's railroad tracks were the wooden rails used in 16th-century England and Europe for horses to pull carts along. In America, wooden rails were first used in 1764 at the Niagara portage in Lewiston, New York. By the time of the Revolutionary War, iron rails were common, but the only power to pull a load along the rails was still horse power.

In 1826 John Stevens built the first successful American steam locomotive in Hoboken, New Jersey, and he was granted the first American railway charter in 1815. On February 28, 1827, the Baltimore & Ohio became the first U.S. railway chartered for the commercial transport of passengers and freight. When the B & O began service in 1830, the track was only 14 miles long, and horses pulled the cars, but development was rapid. In 1831 the steam locomotive *Tom Thumb* replaced the horses and the locomotive *DeWitt Clinton* covered the 17 miles between Albany and Schenectady, New York, in less than an hour. Later that same year a locomotive in Baltimore reached the unheard of speed of 30 miles an hour. By 1860 there were about 30,000 miles of track in the country east of the Mississippi. The railway era had begun.

Throughout the 1850s surveys were made to determine the best route for a railway to California. Several routes looked feasible, but the northern routes were unacceptable to the southern states and the southern routes unacceptable to the northern states. Congress made no decision on which route to fund. But one survey indicated that the best route for a southern railway was through the northern part of Mexico, and Congress was prepared to make this route possible by authorizing the Gadsden Purchase from Mexico.

During the Civil War, President Lincoln was convinced that a railway was needed to encourage settlement in the West, link California with the nation and provide a means of rapid transport for the military. He supported the Pacific Railway Act of 1862 in order to subsidize its construction. Congress authorized vast

land grants to the railways for every mile of track completed as well as cash subsidies of $16,000 per mile of track for easy grades, $32,000 for more difficult sections and $48,000 per mile in the mountains. With these incentives, the Union Pacific Railway was formed to build the line westward and the Central Pacific to build the line to the east from California. When the two lines met at Promontory, Utah, on May 10, 1869, the era of the stagecoach and the wagon trail had come to an end. The three cent stamp honoring the First Transcontenental Railroad was issued in 1944 to mark the 75th anniversary.

On June 4, 1876, the Transcontinental Express arrived in San Francisco only a bit more than 83 hours after leaving New York. Before the railway, that journey, either overland or by ship, would have taken months. Not only were trains going farther but they were going faster. In 1868 the New York to Boston run took 9 hours; by 1881 it took only 7 hours; and by 1892 only a little over 5 hours. The trip from New York to Chicago took 37 hours in 1868, 26 hours and 40 minutes in 1881, and only 24 hours and 45 minutes in 1892. The *Empire State Express*, one of the fastest trains at the time, covered the 440 miles between New York City and Buffalo, New York, at an average speed of 50.77 miles per hour. The iron horse, as the Indians called the train, had bound the nation together with a web of steel.

The Railroad

This early photograph of a Utah Central Railroad engine crossing a wooden trestle on the line between Ogden and Salt Lake bears an almost perfect resemblance to the three cent stamp issued in 1869 when the railroad had just linked the continent from coast to coast. The railroad not only carried people and goods, it seemed to capture something of the very spirit of adventure and progress that characterized the nation in the second half of the 19th century. As the railroad reached more and more communities and dominated the transportation of the nation, it also changed the way we thought about time and distance. Because of its speed, people began to think about travel time in hours rather than days and weeks. To accommodate train schedules the country had to be divided into time zones as the train raced the sun westward far faster than had ever been possible before. Running the railroad "on time" was critical. The timetable told passengers exactly, to the minute, when the train would leave and when it would arrive. Trains ran both ways on a single track so switches had to be opened and closed precisely at the right time. The magic and the speed of the railroad conquered distance and exerted a fascination on the nation. Even in this age of ubiquitous air travel, the train still seems, somehow, the most civilized and romantic way to travel.

Henry Ford

This early photograph of Henry Ford and his young son Edsel sitting proudly in a rare Model F in 1905 captures the pride and self-assurance of the man who revolutionized transportation around the world. Not only did Ford perfect the automobile and turn it from a toy for the rich to a necessity for the common man, he revolutionized the way the factory worked. His assembly line technology produced 15 million Model T Fords between 1908 and 1927 when production was finally stopped. At the height of production, the main assembly plant in Michigan was turning out a Model T every three minutes. Ford paid his workers $5.00 a day – about twice the going rate – and fueled the desire for a better life by providing a car people could afford and a job that paid enough to buy one. In 1900 the car was still a dream that existed largely on paper and the horse and wagon ruled the roads. Twenty years later the horse and wagon were but a memory, and cars and trucks packed the streets. With the ownership of millions of cars came a demand for better roads and with better roads came the ability to live outside the city in the spacious new suburbs. This stamp was issued July 30, 1968.

Overland Mail

From the earliest days of settlement there was a recognition of the need for a reliable communication system with England and Europe and between the various colonies themselves. As early as 1639 a postal service was established between Massachusetts, England and Europe. Richard Fairbanks's tavern in Boston was designated as the place where mail could be sent or received. By 1673 a monthly postal service operated between New York and Boston, and in 1683 William Penn established the first Pennsylvania Post Office.

A royal grant from King William III of England established an official postal system in the American colonies in 1692. In 1737 Benjamin Franklin was appointed postmaster in Philadelphia, and by the outbreak of the Revolutionary War, regular mail service had been established throughout the colonies as well as to Canada and England.

In 1775 the Second Continental Congress authorized the appointment of a postmaster general at a salary of $1,000 a year and the establishment of a line of post offices "from Falmouth in New England to Savannah in Georgia." Although service was slow and delivery times were at the mercy of weather and road conditions, the postal service was the most important, and often the only, system of communication available. By 1788, 2,400 miles of post roads were in use and 75 post offices served a population of 4.5 million. By 1822 service had improved to the point that it took only 11 days to deliver mail from Washington, D.C., to Nashville, Tennessee.

From 1785 to 1845 carriers who used stagecoaches were given priority in obtaining contracts to deliver the mail. Horses were faster and cheaper than stagecoaches for mail delivery, but they did not help the movement of people and goods. Obtaining a contract to carry the mail was an incentive for each new transportation system as the country developed. The post office grew along with the nation, and by 1831 postal employees accounted for more than 75 percent of the civilian workforce of the Federal Government. There were more postmasters than soldiers in the army.

Regular mail service was established to California shortly after it became a state. Mail went by ship from New York to Panama, overland across Panama and then again by ship up the Pacific Coast to San Francisco. The target time of three to four weeks for delivery from New York to San Francisco was frequently not met. In 1858 an overland mail service was established between Tipton, Missouri, and San Francisco. Even though the advertised time was 24 days, the mail often took months to arrive.

To improve service, the famed Pony Express was established to carry mail from St. Joseph, Missouri, to

Sacramento, California, a distance of nearly 2,000 miles. Beginning on April 3, 1860, riders covered 75 to 100 miles a day, changing horses at relay stations every 10 to 15 miles. President Lincoln's Inaugural Address was carried to California in the record time of 7 days, 17 hours. Costs were high, as much as $5 a half-ounce, but the company still did not make a profit. The Pony Express ceased operations on October 26, 1861, the day the transcontinental telegraph line was completed and crucial messages could be sent across the nation almost instantly. Although the telegraph provided an alternative to the mail for short and urgent communications, the postal services continued to expand and their importance increased. By 1860 there were 28,498 post offices; by 1900 they numbered 76,688.

Until 1864 mail was delivered only from post office to post office and people had to pick up their own mail. Home delivery, which originated in England, was soon adopted in the United States. Two deliveries a day were standard in large cities by the 1880s. In 1890, 65 percent of Americans lived in rural areas and still had to go into town to collect their mail. In 1902, to the delight of farmers across the nation, rural free delivery became a permanent feature. Rural populations were now much less isolated from the events of the world, and with the introduction of mail order cataloges, the wonders of big city shopping transformed life on even the most isolated farm.

From 1885 until 1932, except for a brief one-cent increase in 1917, the rate to mail a one-ounce letter anywhere in the United States was two cents. From 1932 to 1958 the rate remained at three cents, making communication and commerce affordable to everyone. The importance of the post office can be measured by the increase in its revenue over the last two centuries: in 1805 revenues amounted to $421,000; in 1905, to over $152 million; and in 2006, to over $72 billion.

Advances in Communication

For two centuries after the Pilgrims stepped ashore in Massachusetts, sending a message over any distance could only be done by writing a letter. With the speed of transportation back and forth between the colonies measured in days and weeks, and between continents often in months, long distance communication was severely limited – sometimes with dire consequences. The Battle of New Orleans between British and American troops, for instance, was fought on January 8, 1815, more than two weeks after the Treaty of Ghent ending the war had been signed. Word of the peace treaty did not arrive in time to prevent the battle and save the lives of its more than 2,000 victims. Such was the state of communication even at the very highest levels. The lack of contact between cities and countries hampered the development of ideas and commerce.

The first major advance toward modern digital communication was Samuel Morse's creation of a single wire telegraph system. Morse code, a system of dots and dashes that were transmitted over telegraph lines by pulses of electrical current, revolutionized long distance communication. The first telegraph line, stretching from Washington to Baltimore, was built with money appropriated by Congress. A quotation from the Bible, "What hath God wrought?" was the first message sent in Morse code over the line on May 24, 1844. Telegraph lines were soon built to link New York with Philadelphia and all the other major cities in the eastern United States. In 1861 Western Union built the first telegraph lines across the continent, thereby putting the Pony Express out of business and binding the nation together with its first communication system that reached from coast to coast. Communication was now a matter of seconds rather than days or weeks.

While the telegraph was a success on land, communication across the ocean still relied on ships to carry letters and documents. The obvious, but difficult, solution was to lay a telegraph cable on the bottom of the ocean. On the fifth attempt, a single cable stretching from Ireland to Newfoundland was successfully laid on August 5, 1858. Service was officially opened on August 16 with the message,

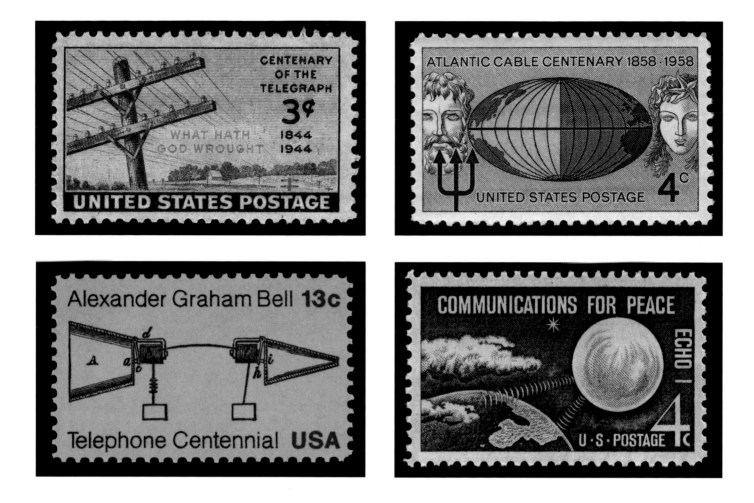

"Glory to God in the highest, and on earth, peace, good will to men." The cable broke down in just a few weeks. In 1866 a more durable cable was laid which worked perfectly. Within 20 years more than 100,000 miles of cable ran along ocean beds linking continents, and rapid communication was possible virtually around the world.

The invention of the telephone, perhaps more than any other advance in personal communications before the Internet, revolutionized the way people kept in touch. Not only was the message communicated, but the person's voice could be heard and, best of all, a conversation could be carried on. It was truly the next best thing to being there. Alexander Graham Bell invented the telephone in 1876. By the middle of 1878 more than 10,000 telephones were already installed and in use. By the end of the century there were an estimated 1.4 million telephones in service. The first coast-to-coast telephone line was completed in 1915 and by 1930 more than 15 million Bell telephones reached into homes across the country.

While the telephone revolutionized how we com-municated on a personal level, it was the radio that united the country. Early radio experiments began in the 1860s and Marconi sent the first successful trans-atlantic message by way of radio waves in 1902, but it was not until the 1920s that radio became reliable and affordable. By 1922 there were about two million radios in private homes and some 500 licensed stations broadcasting. During the Depression, the radio was the one free popular entertainment and the number of listeners skyrocketed. In 1939 there were almost 1,500 stations broadcasting, and 95 percent of American homes had a radio by 1945.

The launch of the first communications satellites in the 1960s again revolutionized the communication industry. The *Echo 1* satellite, put into orbit on August 12, 1960, was a passive solar balloon about 100 feet in diameter. Made of polyester film, it bounced reflected radio, television and telephone signals to ground stations around the world. Although much more sophisticated communication satellites soon filled the skies, *Echo 1* linked the world together and set the stage for the satellite communications systems we have today.

The Open Road

Since colonial times, Americans have been on the move across the continent, and the freedom of the open road has been a part of the American dream. In the period from 1790 to 1840, private toll roads, called turnpikes, greatly improved transportation in the east. In New England over 200 corporations built some 3,700 miles of toll roads but few showed a profit, often because many road users avoided the tollgates, located about every 10 miles along the way. Stagecoaches, so called because tired horses had to be exchanged for fresh horses at predetermined "stages" along the way, were the first overland transportation vehicles for public use. By 1795 more than 20 coaches were making regular trips between Boston and New Haven.

But most roads were in very poor condition and real improvement only came with the automobile. Cars were useless without good roads, and the phenomenal growth of personal car ownership led to a demand for road improvements in every corner of the nation. The automobile revolutionized transportation at an unprecedented rate. In 1900 the horse and wagon was the only means of non-rail overland transportation, and millions were in use everyday. Twenty years later they had virtually disappeared from everyday use in most cities across the country.

1953 Studebaker Starliner   USA 37

In 1903 Henry Ford incorporated the Ford Motor Company with $28,000 in capital. Five years later, Ford introduced the Model T, and in its first full year of production about 18,000 of these sturdy cars were built. By 1912 that figure had jumped to 170,000 a year. The introduction of the assembly line in 1913 pushed the figure to 202,000.

In 1914 Ford began paying his workers $5.00 a day for an eight-hour day, five days a week, about double the going rate for manufacturing jobs at the time. The result was a huge decrease in employee turnover on the assembly line and a corresponding increase in productivity. Ford had realized that his employees were also his market. Workers now had enough money to buy cars and more leisure time to enjoy them. By 1919 half the cars in the United States were Model T's. More than a million were built in 1920 alone, and the word "Ford" was almost synonymous with "car."

Passenger railway traffic immediately felt the impact of the automobile, falling as much as 40 percent between 1920 and 1930. Automobiles opened up the countryside to city dwellers, who had previously had no viable way to travel very far beyond their destination railway stations. In 1929 three times as many people visited the National Parks than in 1920, and 90 percent of them arrived by automobile. Cars also made suburbs and shopping centers possible. And these, located miles from where most people worked, made car ownership a necessity rather than a luxury.

The *New York Times* reported that at the end of 1921 approximately 10 million automobiles were in use in the United States. The 754,000 vehicles registered in New York State alone included 515,773 cars, 140,255 commercial cars and trucks, and 31,915 omnibuses. Total licensing revenue to the state was $9,686,561, a very considerable sum at the time.

As the number of cars grew, vast stretches of land were paved over to create ribbons of concrete linking virtually every city and town in the nation in a way that had not been possible before. Roads could go almost anywhere. Settlement was no longer restricted by the location of rivers and lakes, or by the limitations of railway lines.

President Eisenhower's Federal-Aid Highway Act in 1956 went even further. It provided for a nationwide system of limited-access superhighways. Today the U.S. highway system consists of more than four million miles of roads and some 600,000 bridges.

2005

1955 Ford Thunderbird   USA 37

The Miracle of Flight

Compared to the horse and wagon, trains and automobiles were fast, comfortable and efficient. Yet it still took days to cross the country. Weather conditions made travel difficult, and empty prairies, long stretches of desert, mountains, flat tires and breakdowns all contributed to the stress – and the adventure – of travel. Trains and automobiles still moved slowly enough that travelers could experience the distinct characteristics and identity of different regions of the country.

In 1903, the same year Henry Ford established the Ford Motor Company, Orville Wright achieved the first powered heavier-than-air flight. From this humble beginning, a flight lasting just 12 seconds and covering 120 feet, sprang the nation's fascination with flight. As with the development of the car, improvements in air travel seemed to happen almost overnight. In 1906 Wilbur Wright took a Wright Flyer to Italy and gave flying lessons. The U.S. Army purchased its first airplane in 1909 for $25,000, and in 1910 the first intercity flight covered the 150 miles from Albany to New York City. In 1911 the first transcontinental flight, from New York to California, arrived after only 82 hours in the air – but the trip had taken 49 days and involved 69 stops and crashes along the way.

During World War I, aircraft were used for observation and combat. Eddie Rickenbacker shot down 26 enemy planes in 1918 to become America's first combat ace. After the war, improvements in airplane design and construction came rapidly. In 1919 the first transatlantic flight conquered the 4,500 miles from Long Island, New York, to Plymouth, England – almost the reverse of the *Mayflower*'s voyage 300 years earlier – with refueling stops in Newfoundland, the Azores and Lisbon. Only four years later, in 1923, the first non-stop transcontinental flight, from New York to California, was in the air for less than 27 hours. A century earlier, 27 days would not have been enough for that journey.

Many young Americans were fascinated by flight. Bessie Coleman was the first black woman to earn a pilot's license. She died in 1926 when the Curtiss Jenny biplane in which she was a passenger flipped over, causing Coleman to fall to her death. But the flight that captured the world's attention more than any other and convinced even the skeptics that the airplane had radically changed the world was Charles Lindbergh's 1927 non-stop solo

U.S. Department
of the Air Force
1947–1997

1997

flight across the Atlantic to Paris. Lindbergh received a hero's welcome on both sides of the ocean and inspired a host of other record-setting flights. Among them was Wally Post's first round-the-world solo flight in 1933, which covered almost 16,000 miles in 7 days, 18 hours and 49 minutes.

In 1930 the first regularly scheduled commercial air service was established between New York City and Los Angeles, and by 1936 the first radio traffic reports were broadcast from the Goodyear Blimp over New York City. Zeppelins offered luxurious passenger service between Europe, the United States and South America. These magnificent machines captured the imagination of the Depression-weary generation until the great *Hindenburg* crashed and burned in New Jersey in 1937.

By this time airplanes had become not only reliable but much faster. In 1936 Howard Hughes set a speed record of 259 miles an hour. By 1939 the

transcontinental flight record was 7 hours and 2 minutes. It was now possible to eat breakfast in New York and dinner in Los Angeles.

The huge improvement in aircraft made during World War II and the perfecting of radar and radio communications led directly to the development of worldwide commercial air travel. The airplane eliminated travelers' concerns about road conditions and the difficulties of crossing mountains, lakes and rivers by simply flying over them. Once a plane was in the air, all earlier obstacles vanished. As speeds increased and ticket prices fell, the barrier of distance between parts of our vast country was virtually eliminated. Catching a plane had become as safe and reliable as hopping on a train. America – and the world itself – had become a global village. The American dream of mobility and easy access to every corner of the nation, and of the world, had finally become a reality.

The *Graf Zeppelin*

The most famous image of these great airships is the fiery crash of the *Hindenburg* in New Jersey in 1937. Another great airship the *Graf Zeppelin*, the Nazi swastika proudly emblazoned on the fins, is shown here flying over New York in May 1936 when these magnificent silent airships ruled the skies. The airship is named after its inventor, Ferdinand Adolf August Heinrich von Zeppelin, born in Germany in 1838. Graf is the German title for a Count. Zeppelin visited America and was a military observer for the Union Army and made his first flight in a balloon while in Minnesota. He was awarded a patent for a Navigable Balloon in 1899 and began a commercial air service in 1908. The Zeppelin had captured the imagination of the nation to such an extent behat when the Empire State Building was opened in New York in

1931, a mooring mast was constructed on top of the building to allow the Zeppelin to dock so its elegant passengers could disembark on the roof. The reality of unpredictable and intense winds blowing around the tallest building in the world made such a landing impossible. This stamp, one of a set of three issued on April 19, 1930, paid for a letter to be carried on the round-trip flight. The regular letter rate to anywhere in the United States was just two cents in 1930 so this was very expensive mail indeed.

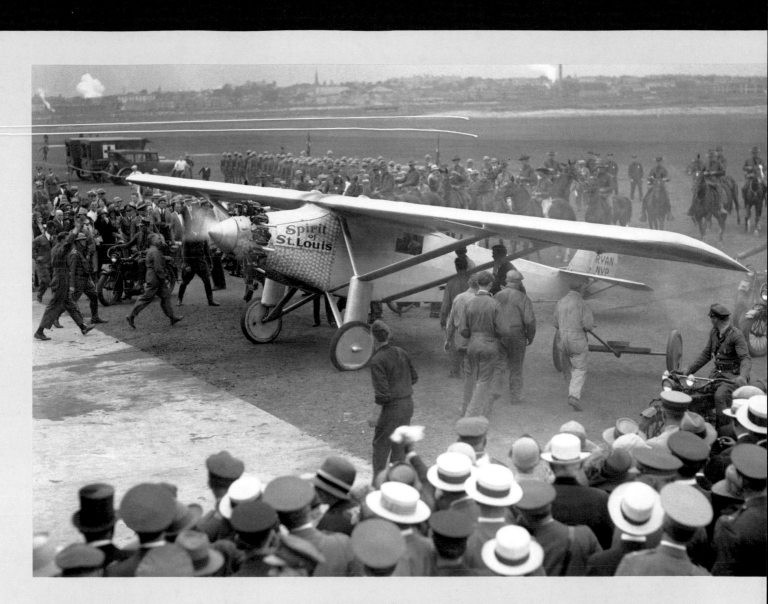

Charles Lindbergh

This photograph shows Charles Lindbergh's famous plane *Spirit of St. Louis* landing in Boston in July, 1927, on the first leg of his tour around the United States after his successful flight to Paris. He had won the $25,000 prize offered for the first flight across the Atlantic to Paris. Lindbergh's 33½-hour non-stop flight demonstrated that the airplane would dominate the future of international travel. Before long, transPacific and around-the-world flights would be made. The technology of flight improved rapidly until time and distance shrank to the point that no place was really remote anymore. Lindbergh went on to become an influential and controversial figure in the United States and in Europe during the 1930s. Lindbergh had been a mail pilot before his historic flight. The United States Post Office purchased an airplane from the Wright brothers and began offering Air Mail service

in 1918. Air Mail service remained an option, at extra cost, until 1977 when the post office abandoned two classes of mail and sent all first-class mail by air whenever possible. Although we now have commuter airlines making many trips a day between major cities, the magic of that first flight from New York to Paris will always remain one of the high points in the history of aviation. This stamp was issued on June 18, 1927.

The Final Frontier

On October 4, 1957, the Soviet Union surprised the world with its launch of *Sputnik*, the first man-made object to orbit the Earth. A month later, even that achievement was dwarfed when *Sputnik 2* was successfully put in orbit. This time the satellite carried a dog and transmitted information back to Earth for three weeks before its batteries failed. Unfortunately, the dog, Laika, did not survive the trip. The space race had begun and the United States was definitely in second place.

Although the United States put *Explorer 1* in orbit a few months later on January 31, 1958, this tiny satellite, weighing only 30.7 pounds, was embarrassing compared to the first *Sputnik*, which weighed 184 pounds. On April 12, 1961, the Soviet Union again achieved a scientific and political victory when it launched Yuri Gagarin into space and returned him safely after a single orbit around the Earth.

On May 25, 1961, at the height of the Cold War, President Kennedy made a special address to Congress. He committed the United States to the most daring mission since the journey of the very first settlers to these shores – putting a man on the moon and bringing him back safely. Not only did this need to be done, he said, but it needed to be done before the end of the decade so that the rest of the world could have renewed confidence in America's leadership of the free world.

> Now it is ... time for a great new American enterprise – time for this nation to take a clearly leading role in space achievement, which in many ways may hold the key to our future on Earth ... I believe that this nation should commit itself to achieving the goal, before this decade is out, of landing a man on the Moon and returning him safely to the Earth. No single space project in this period will be more impressive to mankind, or more important for the long-range exploration of space; and none will be so difficult or expensive to accomplish ... But in a very real sense, it will not be one man going to the Moon ... it will be an entire nation. For all of us must work to put him there.

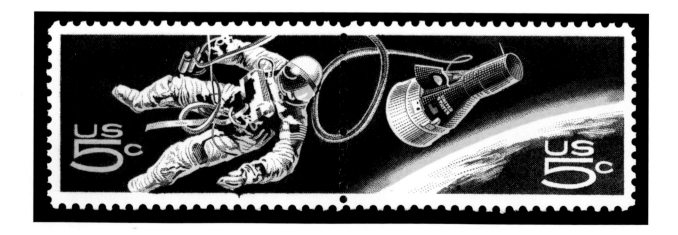

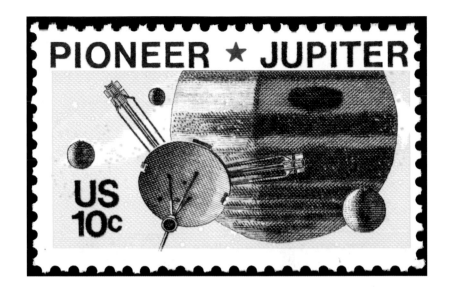

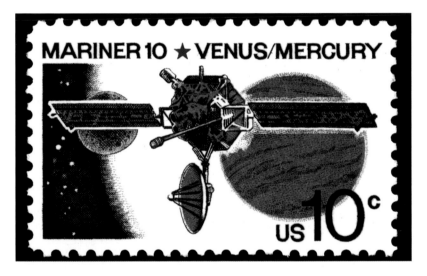

US **10**c

APOLLO SOYUZ 1975

4^c *U.S. MAN IN SPACE*

PROJECT MERCURY

US 10c

Skylab

And so began preparations for the most high-profile and the most perilous voyage into the unknown ever attempted. Space, the final frontier, was about to begin giving up its secrets.

On July 20, 1969, just a few months before President Kennedy's deadline of the end of the decade, Neil Armstrong became the first man to set foot on the moon. His words, "One small step for man; one giant leap for mankind," have become inscribed in national memory.

The conquest of space demonstrated that there seems to be little, if anything, the country cannot accomplish if it puts its mind to it. There were, of course, setbacks and failures, as well as the tragic loss of astronauts' lives, but the 1960s and 1970s will be remembered as one of the greatest ages of exploration in the history of the world.

By the time the Apollo Program ended in 1975, 12 men had stood on the moon. NASA then turned its attention to the development of a reusable space shuttle. The Shuttle Orbiters can make trips just outside Earth's orbit and were specifically designed for carrying cargo into orbit. The craft proved ideal for satellite launch and repair, and for building the Space Station. Although six Orbiters have been built, *Enterprise*, named after the famous craft on the television program *Star Trek*, was only a test vehicle and not equipped for space flight. Two Orbiters were lost on mission: *Challenger* exploded shortly after takeoff in 1986 and *Columbia* was lost on reentry in 2003. *Atlantis*, *Discovery* and *Endeavour* continue to fly but after the loss of *Columbia*, the decision was made to complete the International Space Station and retire the Shuttle fleet by 2010. The current vision for space exploration calls for the development of a new Crew Exploration Vehicle (CEV) to replace the Shuttle and be in service by 2014. America, and the world, awaits the next step in the exploration of space.

The First Man on the Moon

This stamp commemorates the fulfillment of the dream first expressed by John F. Kennedy in 1961 when he proposed that the United States should dedicate itself to the goal of putting a man on the moon and returning him safely to Earth before the end of the decade. Although Kennedy did not live to see it, Neil Armstrong became the first man to set foot on the moon on July 20, 1969. It was the greatest moment in the history of exploration since Columbus sighted land in 1492. Armstrong's words when the lunar module touched down safely — "The Eagle has landed" — and his first words when he stepped onto the surface of the moon itself — "That's one small step for man, one giant leap for mankind" — have become part of our language and our history. This photo of Armstrong setting foot on the surface as he climbs down from the lunar module served as the model for the drawing on the stamp that also shows the Earth floating in space as it appears from the moon. Six more lunar landings

took place before this phase of our space program came to an end in 1972. Many stamps were issued to commemorate America's achievements in space, but none was so dramatic or so filled with emotion as this unforgettable moment in America's history. This stamp was issued on September 9, 1969.

Space Shuttle *Endeavour*

Unlike the great rockets that launched the astronauts on their journey to the moon, the Space Shuttle was designed to make repeated journeys to the edge of space and deliver cargo into low orbit around the Earth. The first Shuttle launch occurred in 1981, and they continue today. Kennedy Space Center in Florida is the site of all Shuttle launches and is one of the most popular tourist attractions in the state. Despite the tragic loss of two orbiters, the Space Shuttle has made possible the International Space Station and the Hubble Space Telescope. The Space Station not only provided valuable lessons in working and living in space but also allowed the United States to partner with the Soviet Union and other nations in a truly international effort, and the Hubble Telescope has amazed the world with its incredible high-definition images of far-away galaxies. The huge, reddish liquid fuel tank provides the power for lift-off and then falls away into the sea where it is recovered and reused. The two white rockets are solid fuel boosters that provide the final power to push the Orbiter into space. At each launch, thousands gather along the coast of Florida to watch the

huge craft weighing four and a half million pounds rise majestically into the air until it disappears from view. This stamp was issued on August 4, 1995.

127

Every gun that is made,
every warship launched,
every rocket fired, signifies a theft
from those who hunger
and are not fed,
those who are cold
and are not clothed.

– Dwight D. Eisenhower

PART 6

THE
GREATEST
GENERATION

THE GREATEST GENERATION

As the 19th century drew to a close, the optimism that had characterized the century of westward expansion still dominated the country. The period 1900–1914 saw the largest number of immigrants on record flood into the country. By the census of 1910, the population of the United States had swollen to over 100 million, and our industrial output exceeded that of any other country in the world. America had grown up. It was no longer a young struggling country busy settling a hostile wilderness. It was a world power about to experience a century in which its wealth and influence, participation and finally domination in world affairs would increase with each passing year. For America – and for the world – the 20th century would be a period of war and preparation for war.

Despite America's size and strength, its army and navy remained small and the country had little interest in the diplomatic and military affairs of Europe and the Far East. When war broke out in August 1914, many in Europe greeted it with enthusiasm. Expecting the hostilities to be short-lived, men rushed to enlist in fear of missing out on the action. There was no hurry. The war dragged on for a full four years. The horror of mud, machine guns, barbed wire and trenches eliminated the best and brightest of an entire generation, redrew the map of Europe, and sowed the seeds of the Great Depression and another war.

America remained neutral in the first years of the carnage, but by 1917 Germany, desperate for victory, had begun to sink any ship found in waters off England in an attempt to stop the flow of supplies to its enemy. The danger, real and imagined, to American shipping, trade and lives came to a head with the sinking of seven U.S. merchant ships by German submarines and the revelation that Germany had urged Mexico to declare war on the United States in the event that the United States went to war with Germany. Although opposition to intervention remained strong in Congress, President Wilson called for a declaration of war against Germany and its allies, and more than four million American men were hastily trained for battle in Europe. Fighting to "make the world safe for democracy" in this "war to end all wars," the American Expeditionary Force provided fresh manpower and unlimited supplies to the exhausted allies. By the time Germany surrendered, more than a 100,000 Americans had been killed, and more than 200,000 had been wounded, taken prisoner or listed as missing in action.

When the armistice was signed on November 11, 1918, the toll of dead and wounded on both sides stood at 21 million, and Europe was physically, mentally and morally exhausted.

America, the major military and industrial power in the world, rejected membership in the League of Nations and withdrew, as much as possible, from the international stage. Its factories undamaged, America surged ahead to prosperity, but, for Americans, the great trials of the 20th century were yet to come.

An American born in 1920 was 9 years old when the stock market crashed and the Great Depression began, 21 when Pearl Harbor was bombed and only 25 when the troop ships returned from Europe and Asia at the end of the war in 1945. Still young, but hardened and matured by experience, the generation of Americans born in the first quarter of the 20th century faced the 1950s with confidence that the worst was over. They had survived the Depression, won the war and, through the United Nations and NATO, were determined to secure the peace. More than anything else America wanted a "return to normalcy" – a time when factories could build cars not tanks.

Confidence in the future and a determination to make up for lost time produced the great baby boom of the 1940s, 50s and 60s. Between 1946 and 1964 more than 75 million babies were born in the United States. Their parents worked and saved to provide them with everything that the Depression and the war had denied their generation. But normalcy, whatever that meant to the many different segments of the population, was not to return. The war had changed the world and America could not, as it had done at the end of World War I, turn its back on world affairs or turn the clock back to a simpler time. Hardly had the fighting ended when America found itself at war in Korea at a time when it was also deeply involved in rebuilding Europe. Two great superpowers, each armed with enough nuclear bombs to annihilate civilization as we know it – if not life itself on the planet – faced each other in an uneasy peace.

Despite the clouds of war, American children born in the baby boom were raised in a time of prosperity and with a sense of entitlement. Unable to grasp the sacrifices their parents had made, they saw the conformity and contentment of their parents' lives as dull and suffocating. The teenagers of the 1960s craved change, personal freedom and excitement. It was as if the pent-up energies of the nation, dormant for three decades since the abrupt end of the roaring twenties, burst out again in the 1960s' counter-culture explosion. America – and the world – had been irrevocably changed. However, for a brief period after 1945, the United States portrayed its values and dreams on a series of stamps that celebrated American accomplishments and illustrated our determination to retain the essential values that continue to define the nation despite the enormous changes that have occurred.

The Great Depression

Fear was the dominant mood in America and around the world when Franklin Delano Roosevelt was sworn in as the 32nd president of the United States on March 4, 1933. On "Black Thursday," October 24, 1929, the greatest stock market crash in history had seen $9 billion wiped from the value of the market and a record 13 million shares traded. The ticker tape reporting the stock prices ran more than an hour late as it carried the bad news across the nation. Although no one realized it at the time, the United States was on the brink of the worst economic depression in its history and faced a decade of economic hardship that would ultimately be relieved only by the demands of war production.

Among the many causes of the Great Depression were a stock market driven by greed rather than reason, a currency that was tied to gold, the practice of buying on margin, the huge debts incurred by all the European powers at the end of the First World War and an unsophisticated financial system simply unable to cope with the magnitude of the problems besetting the world economy. In 1931 some 2,300 banks in the United States closed their doors. By 1932 more than 10 million Americans were out of work and many more had only part-time jobs or were working for reduced wages. International trade, on which America depended for its markets, withered away as nation after nation fell victim to the Depression. In 1929 the value of U.S. international trade stood at about $36 billion; by 1932 it had dropped by two-thirds to only $12 billion.

Americans looked to the incoming president to save them. In his Inaugural Address Roosevelt faced the problem squarely and reassured Americans that he understood their suffering and would take the kind of decisive action usually reserved for a time of war:

> Let me assert my firm belief that the only thing we have to fear is fear itself ... Our greatest primary task is to put people to work ... In our progress toward a resumption of work ... there must be a strict supervision of all banking and credits and investments; there must be an end to speculation with other people's money ... It is to be hoped that the normal balance of executive and legislative authority may be wholly adequate to meet the unprecedented task before us ... [If not] ... I shall ask the Congress for ... broad Executive power to wage a war against the emergency, as great as the power that would be given to me if we were in fact invaded by a foreign foe.

Despite the best efforts of Roosevelt's revolutionary New Deal, however, the economic problems were resistant to any quick solution. The Depression was to last for a decade. But the American people learned to cope and to adjust to drastically limited opportunity. Especially in the first years of the Depression, many commentators noted how stoically the people seemed to accept the situation. In the face of tremendous suffering and hardship, Americans pulled together and the government's intervention in the economy, as these stamps show, brought about some long-term benefits. The Tennessee Valley Authority reduced flooding and provided irrigation and power to much of the south, and the Rural Electrification Administration took electrical power to the most remote corners of the nation. The Civilian Conservation Corps provided employment for millions of young men, who planted trees and worked to restore

the land across the country. And by picking up the baton to host the Olympic Games in 1932, America provided a way in which the nation and the world could take their minds off their troubles.

Franklin Delano Roosevelt

During his unprecedented four terms in office, Franklin Delano Roosevelt addressed the nation by radio many times. Although his legislation was often controversial, his genuine concern for the common man is unquestioned and it was to the common man that this 1938 radio address was aimed. Sitting behind a desk facing a bank of microphones the President, resplendent in crisp white shirt and bow tie, explained to the people the proposal he had just put before Congress asking for an increase in the money for job creation and relief. At the end of his talk he reassured the people that he had not forgotten them or their suffering: "And finally I should like to say a personal word to you. I never forget that I live in a house owned by all the American people ... I seek to look beyond the doors of the White House ... into the hopes and fears of men and women in their homes ... I try not to forget that what really counts at the bottom of it all is that the men and women willing to work can have a decent job ... I know that I must never give up – that I must never let the ... people down." Conditions might be difficult but the familiar, compassionate voice over the radio gave America the sense that we would come through into better times. This stamp was issued on January 30, 1982.

Eleanor Roosevelt

In this photograph taken at the height of the Depression in 1935, Eleanor Roosevelt talks to a young girl while visiting a public works slum clearance project in Detroit. To Americans in the 1930s and 1940s, Eleanor Roosevelt was much more than the wife of the President – she was a woman of immense influence and energy who brought her genuine interest in people and her natural sense of social justice to work for men and women everywhere. She traveled widely, spoke directly to people in need across the country, wrote a newspaper column, "My Day," which appeared daily from 1935 to 1962 and, at the height of her popularity, was syndicated in over 90 newspapers around the country. Throughout his Presidency, Franklin Roosevelt depended on his wife to be his eyes and ears around the nation. Like her husband, Eleanor Roosevelt personified a leader with a genuine concern for the needy. She gave people hope in a difficult time and worked tirelessly to ensure that greater social justice, as well as material prosperity, would be her legacy. Appointed the American spokesperson in the United Nations, she was the recipient of many honors and awards during her life. Eleanor Roosevelt remains a symbol of what one person can do to make this a better world. This stamp was issued on October 11, 1984.

World War II

When war in Europe began again in September 1939, a *New York Times* opinion poll indicated that 65 percent of the population believed that America should not become involved. Nevertheless, throughout 1940 and 1941 the American government began tentatively to prepare for war and to provide aid to Britain. But the deep scars of the Depression still lingered. Jobs and economic security remained the primary concerns of most Americans, and the war in Europe still seemed far away.

All opposition to America's participation in the war vanished on December 7, 1941, "a day that shall live in infamy" as President Roosevelt called it, when Japanese forces attacked Pearl Harbor without warning. Congress immediately passed a declaration of war against Japan by a vote of 470 to 1. On December 11 Germany declared war on the United States, and America found itself committed to fighting on the other side of both the Atlantic and Pacific Oceans at the same time. Although America would again be spared the destruction of the battleground, which

reduced much of Europe to rubble for the second time in a century, World War II claimed over 400,000 American casualties and saw the entire economy transformed as the nation mobilized for war. America was truly the "arsenal of democracy," not only supplying its own army with millions upon millions of items needed for the 16 million men in service but also sending millions of tons of arms and supplies to its major allies, Britain, Canada and Russia.

In 1941 Britain stood alone in the west while Russia bore the full force of the German invasion in June. American troops landed in Africa in November 1942, and then in Italy in July 1943, before participating in the great D-Day invasion at Normandy in France in June 1944. By March 1945, the Allied armies under Supreme Commander Dwight D. Eisenhower had crossed the Rhine and invaded Germany itself. Russian forces reached Berlin in April 1945, and Germany surrendered unconditionally on May 7, 1945. Europe was free of the Nazi terror, but it lay in

ruins, with tens of millions dead and its transportation, housing, agricultural and industrial infrastructure destroyed.

In the Pacific, unlike in Europe where Russian, British and Canadian troops bore much of the fighting, the Americans fought virtually alone with supply lines stretching over 3,000 miles of water. Under General Douglas MacArthur the Americans first halted the Japanese advance and then slowly and methodically pushed them back across the Pacific to the shores of Japan itself. The major battles were fought on the sea, in the air and on the islands. Given the determination of Japanese soldiers to fight virtually to the last man in the invasion of Iwo Jima and other islands, the casualty estimates for any attempt to invade and conquer Japan itself rose to a million Americans and millions more Japanese killed.

The creation of the atomic bomb offered a terrible alternative to invasion. With the proof of what this weapon of mass destruction could do demonstrated

on the cities of Hiroshima and Nagasaki, the Japanese surrendered on September 2, 1945. The war was over in the Pacific too, and the world was finally at peace.

The Soviet Union, however, soon changed from an ally to an adversary as the Iron Curtain closed over the European nations it had occupied during the war. The development of a Soviet atomic bomb added power to what, at the end of the war, was the largest standing army in the world with over 25 million men under arms, and made the Soviet Union the second great world power. At the outset of the war George Bernard Shaw had predicted that there would

be only two winners at the end of the war, the United States and the Soviet Union. He was correct.

The stamps shown here portray the two American generals, Eisenhower and MacArthur, who led American forces in Europe and the Pacific respectively, as well as Winston Churchill, who inspired the English during the dark days of 1940 and 1941 when England stood alone against Hitler, and then led them to victory. The army, navy, coast guard, merchant marine and women in our armed forces stamps were issued to recognize the Americans who had served throughout the war.

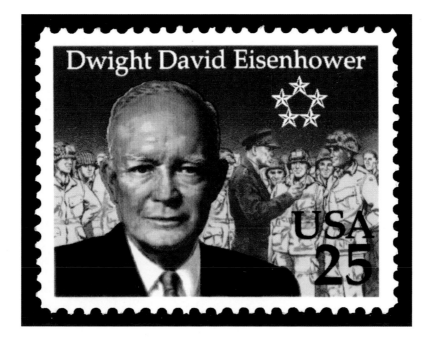

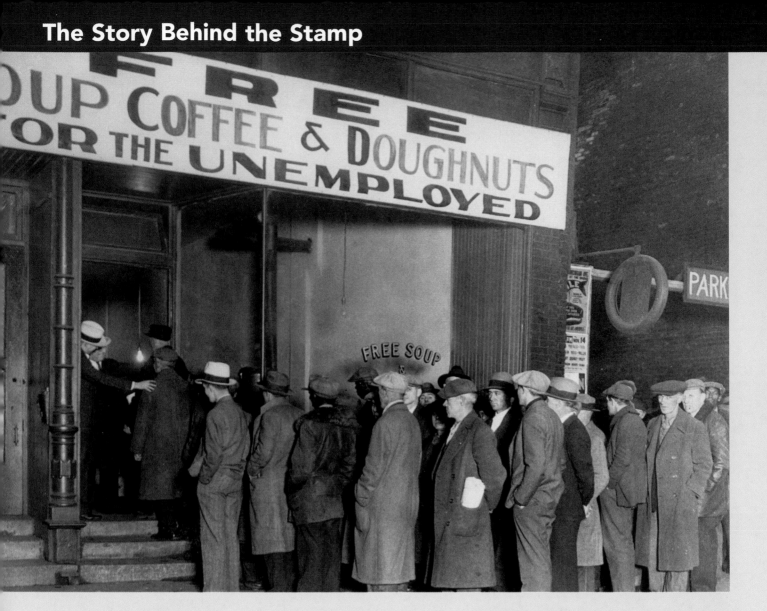

The Great Depression

This photograph shows the reality of the Great Depression in Chicago. The long line of unemployed men stretches down the street and out of the photograph. Some are in working clothes but others are in the suits they wore to the office before their jobs disappeared. All are orderly, resigned somehow to their fate. The man at the door in a tie and white shirt greets them with a welcoming hand on the shoulder. All want and need the free soup, coffee and doughnuts available here. This scene was, unfortunately, common across the nation during the 1930s. About 3,500 people a day were fed here at a cost of $300 a day. What makes this photograph different is that the storefront coffee shop was a public relations gesture by Al Capone, the famous Chicago bootlegger and gangster who was later sentenced to 11 years in prison for tax evasion. The National Recovery Act stamp shows the people of the nation – farmers, office workers, laborers and women – "united in common determination" to make things better. The NRA attempted to regulate factory wages and production to maintain employment but was declared unconstitutional by the Supreme Court because the government had no power to enact such legislation. In the language of the Court: "Extraordinary conditions do not create or enlarge constitutional power."

Nonetheless, the nation's "common determination" was the mark of an entire generation doomed to survive the long years of a depression that ultimately was only relieved by war. This stamp was issued on August 15, 1933.

Iwo Jima

The men in this photograph are part of the 70,000 Marines who took part in the invasion of the island of Iwo Jima that began on February 19, 1945. The Japanese had dug an extensive system of tunnels into the island that protected them from the intense bombardment and shelling from naval guns that preceded the invasion. The Japanese fought to the death to defend the island. 26,000 Americans and 21,000 Japanese were either killed or wounded in savage fighting that lasted for 36 days before the Marines finally captured the tiny eight-square-mile island fortress. The capture of Iwo Jima was a part of America's island hopping strategy in the Pacific. The Japanese were forced to retreat to bases closer and closer to Japan but only after bitter fighting each step of the way. The stamp shows the Marines raising the flag on Mount Suribachi on Iwo Jima is one of the most famous images from World War II. After the war, sculptor Felix W. de Weldon constructed a bronze sculpture of the scene. The memorial, standing 32 feet high, was dedicated by President Eisenhower on November 10, 1954 on the 179th anniversary of the founding of the U.S. Marine Corps. A cloth flag flies from the pole 24 hours a day and the base of the memorial is inscribed with the words of Admiral Nimitz's tribute to the fighting men on Iwo Jima: "Uncommon Valor was a Common Virtue." This stamp was issued on July 11, 1945.

No Greater Sacrifice

The peace achieved in 1945, unfortunately, was to be short-lived. Just five years after the surrender of Japan, tensions between Russia and China and the Western powers exploded in Korea. The border between North and South Korea had been established when Russian armies invaded the north in the last days of the war, as Japan withdrew. In 1950 the North Korean army crossed the 38th parallel and invaded South Korea. While fighting under the United Nations flag, more than 35,000 Americans were killed in this "police action," which succeeded only in holding the border between North and South Korea at the 38th parallel, precisely where it had been when the war started.

The growing might of both Russia and China in the aftermath of Korea put America virtually on a war footing for most of the Cold War in fear, as Nikita Khrushchev put it so succinctly, that: "Whether you like it or not, history is on our side. We will bury you."

The next major military conflict to involve the United States, the Vietnam War, also had its origins in an artificial north-south border, this one drawn when rebel troops supported by China drove the French out of Vietnam. Convinced that South Vietnam could not survive a war with North Vietnam, President Kennedy began sending in more military advisers in 1961. As the fighting escalated, so did U.S. participation, and America found itself trapped in a land war in Asia.

Vietnam became for America a lesson that sophisticated modern armies could not win a guerrilla war against a low-tech army fighting on their own ground. As the war ground on in Asia, mounting casualties, massive costs, and dissension and opposition at home at last convinced the government to pull out of Vietnam. It was the first war that America had lost, and it was a bitter lesson about intervening in civil wars in different cultures far from home.

Although the legacy and lessons of Vietnam still linger, the collapse of the Soviet Union and the transformation of China from an impoverished agrarian nation into one of America's largest trading partners have greatly reduced tensions. Yet the need to protect America's global interests continues.

The sacrifices and loyalty shown by the nation's military personnel during this most difficult of times have been honored and recorded on many stamps. The National World War II Memorial and the Vietnam Veterans Memorial in Washington, D.C., are visited by millions of Americans each year. The Military Academy at West Point, the World War II Memorial and the Vietnam Veterans Memorial are honored on these stamps, as well as recipients of the Medal of Honor, the highest award for valor in action that can be given to an individual serving in the Armed Forces of the United States. The "dog tags" and flag on the 32 cent stamp honor those who were taken prisoners of war (POW) or are officially listed as missing in action (MIA). All of these stamps pay tribute to the men and women who have served their nation in the military, and especially those who have paid the ultimate price and shown that "no greater love hath any man than to lay down his life for another."

37USA

NATIONAL WORLD WAR II MEMORIAL
2004

Vietnam Veterans Memorial USA 20c

POW & MIA
NEVER FORGOTTEN

32
USA

USA 20c
Medal of Honor

Truly Extraordinary Change

The man on the stamp and the man in the photograph are father and son. Benjamin Davis, Sr. served for 50 years in positions of increasing responsibility but was always posted to positions that would not put him in command of white troops or officers. He was promoted to brigadier general in 1940. The War Department citation awarding him the Distinguished Service Medal noted his "exceptionally meritorious service ... on matters pertaining to Negro troops." Davis, Jr. was determined to overcome the prejudice that had limited his father's career. As the only black cadet at West Point he had no roommate and ate his meals alone. No white cadets would speak to him except for official reasons. This prejudice only made him more determined to succeed and he graduated near the top of his class in 1936. In 1940 Davis, Jr. took command of America's first black military air unit at Tuskegee Air Force Base, Alabama. The Tuskegee Airmen flew 15,000 combat sorties, earned 150 Distinguished Flying Crosses, 744 Air Medals, 8 Purple Hearts and 14 Bronze Stars. Davis flew sixty missions himself and among other awards earned the Silver Star, Legion of Merit and Distinguished Flying Cross. After the war Benjamin Davis, Jr. rose to the rank of General. In 1970 he retired from the air force after 33 years on active duty. At his funeral, President Clinton said that Davis was proof that "through example and perseverance, one person can bring truly extraordinary change." These words apply to both father and son. This stamp was issued on January 28, 1997.

The Four Chaplains

On January 23, 1943 the *USS Dorchester* left New York and joined a convoy bound for Greenland. The night of February 3 she was torpedoed by a German submarine and sank in less than 20 minutes with a loss of some 675 men out of a total of 902 aboard. It was the third largest loss of men at sea for the United States in World War II.

As the ship began to sink the four chaplains distributed life jackets to those in need and reassured men on the verge of panic. When the supply of life jackets ran out, the chaplains gave their own life jackets to others. This unselfish action doomed them to certain death in the frigid waters. As the ship slid beneath the waves, the four chaplains were seen to link arms and pray together in a lasting symbol of heroism and interfaith unity in the service of their common God.

Charter members of the Greatest Generation, these four men were true heroes: George L. Fox – a Methodist minister; Alexander D. Goode – a Jewish rabbi; Clark V. Poling – a Dutch Reformed minister;

and John P. Washington – a Catholic priest.

In 1960 Congress created the Four Chaplains Medal to honor these men. It is a civilian rather than military decoration and is intended to rank just below the Congressional Medal of Honor, America's highest military decoration. The photograph shows the chaplains' next of kin receiving citations in 1945. This stamp was issued on May 28, 1948.

The Cold War

With the death of Franklin D. Roosevelt on April 12, 1945, less than a month before the end of the war in Europe, the nation faced the end of a presidency that had lasted so long it was the only one that many young people could remember. Roosevelt had been elected for an unprecedented third and fourth term and had guided the country successfully through the Depression and the war. But his unique four terms in office made it a certainty that the transition to a new face in the White House, like the transition to peace itself, would be difficult. The stamps shown here offer a look at the state of mind of postwar America.

The Atoms for Peace issue of 1955 expressed the greatest desire of a generation of Americans preoccupied with fallout shelters and drills instructing school children to hide under their desks in the event of a nuclear attack. It would have done no good at all to be under a desk in a war in which the living would envy the dead, but the stamp reminded us all that the oceans were no deterrent to missile-based atomic bombs. The war would never again be "over there."

Much of our hope for peace was placed in the postwar organizations of the United Nations and the North Atlantic Treaty Organization (NATO). Determined not to repeat the failure of the League of Nations, America welcomed the United Nations to a permanent home in New York as well as joining with the nations of Europe to establish an alliance in which an attack by the Soviet Union on any one of them would constitute an attack on all. At home the returning soldiers joined the American Legion and the Veterans of Foreign Wars and enlisted in the Armed Forces Reserve to provide a pool of men ready to be called on in time of need.

The willingness of Americans to help rebuild individual lives as well as entire nations was commemorated on the World Refugee Year stamp. Between 1948 and 1952 American contributions to Europe's recovery totaled over $13 billion. America was committed to sharing its bounty with former allies and enemies alike, and wanted to ensure that all the nations devastated by war had the opportunity to restore democratic systems of government. America's willingness to provide a military shield and the money necessary to rebuild their countries gave Europe a chance to rejoin the community of nations.

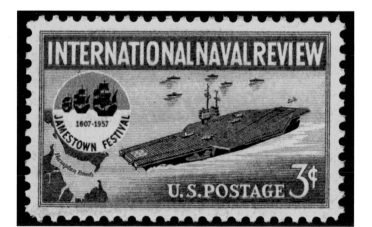

Children Are the Future

Along with their push to traverse the continent, build an industrial and military power greater than the world has ever known, and excel in business and industry, Americans have retained a strong sense of family values and social responsibility.

From the nation's earliest days, education has been considered important for preparing a people called upon every four years to intelligently make decisions and vote. American pioneers had to cope with danger and deprivation in the wilderness, but they established churches and schools as soon after settlement as possible. Harvard, the oldest university in America, graduated its first class in 1642, just 22 years after the arrival of the Pilgrims. The value Americans place on the virtues of hard work, cooperation and communal effort, which we associate with the independent farmer, has led to our idealization of the small town and the frontier as the places providing the greatest opportunity for all. This reliance on faith, social values and education has endured and has contributed to making America a world leader in many fields today.

These pages present some of the most appealing of all United States stamps, vignettes depicting the hopes of all Americans for the great baby boom generation. They celebrate the spirit and potential of the youth of America. Children benefited, for the first time in history, from modern dental care right from childhood; many followed in their parents' footsteps on family farms, and, most of all, they had a chance to get a good education. Parents who had been unable to finish high school or college during the Depression and the war were determined to let nothing get in the way of their children being all that they could be. The stamp honoring the teachers of America shows clean and well-dressed students eager to learn, as does the Youth Month issue, in which two young people stride confidently ahead, schoolbooks tucked under their arms.

New colleges and universities as well as apprenticeship programs were established to ensure a prosperous future for America's youth. In addition, the space race with the Soviet Union, beginning with the launch of *Sputnik* in 1957 and America's subsequent commitment to putting a man on the moon, sparked a great re-evaluation of the education system, especially programs in the sciences and engineering. Whatever the reason for the emphasis on education throughout our history, the fulfillment of the dream of the Greatest Generation can be seen in the unprecedented numbers of college graduates in these postwar years.

U.S. POSTAGE 3¢

1928 FUTURE FARMERS OF AMERICA 1953

HONORING THE TEACHERS OF AMERICA

NATIONAL EDUCATION ASSOCIATION 1857 1957

UNITED STATES POSTAGE 3¢

AMERICAN DENTAL ASSOCIATION 1859-1959

Dental Health

UNITED STATES POSTAGE 4¢

SALUTING YOUNG AMERICA

YOUTH MONTH SEPT. 1-30, 1948

3¢ UNITED STATES POSTAGE 3¢

4¢ U.S. POSTAGE

GIRL SCOUTS • U.S.A.

3¢ U.S. POSTAGE

IN RECOGNITION OF THE IMPORTANT SERVICE RENDERED THEIR COMMUNITIES AND THEIR NATION BY AMERICA'S NEWSPAPERBOYS

BUSY BOYS ... BETTER BOYS

FREE ENTERPRISE

Labor Is Life

America is the land of opportunity. Here there is no entrenched nobility owning the land, no class system and no hereditary rights. Abraham Lincoln was born in a log cabin and rose to become President; Andrew Carnegie rose from poverty to become one of the richest men in the world. But much more impressive than these dramatic examples of self-made success, were the millions of men and women who arrived on these shores with nothing and, through hard work and determination, built a home, raised a family, educated their children, put away savings, and retired with dignity. The American dream is not a rags to riches story, but a story of success at the grass roots level by generation after generation of immigrants who asked nothing more of their new nation than the chance to find work.

Organized labor was the voice of the worker in the struggle for a just and equitable distribution of wealth. It took strikes, dedication and suffering to organize workers and achieve better working conditions. Labor Day is honored with a stamp proclaiming "Labor is Life" and features a man shouldering the tools of his trade as his wife instructs their child from the book on her knee. This scene represents the dignity of labor when there is hope for a better future for the next generation – a defining quality of the American dream.

Samuel Gompers, the first president of the newly formed American Federation of Labor in 1886, and George Meany, who unified two major union organizations into the AFL-CIO in 1955 and became its first president, are each honored on a stamp. The stamps honoring the centenary of the steel industry and banking and commerce recognize that, for working people to prosper, the industrial base of the nation must be sound.

Health and Medicine

The medical advances made in the 20th century have conquered ailments that have plagued humanity since the dawn of time. Smallpox, diphtheria, polio, leprosy and tuberculosis have been eradicated from the United States and most of the world, and standards of public health care have been greatly improved. Scientific advances in the prevention and treatment of disease, better nutrition and early diagnosis have all combined to produce an improvement in the general health of the population undreamed of only a few generations ago. Nevertheless, there remains much to do. Heart disease and cancer are still major problems that strike millions of Americans each year.

These stamps honor just a few of the most important achievements in health and medicine. The American Red Cross, begun 1881, is honored with a stamp showing founder Clara Barton looking at a globe that symbolizes the organization's worldwide mission. The Mayo brothers pioneered group practice in medicine, and the cancer stamp bears the important message – early diagnosis saves lives.

The Postmaster General said the Prevent Drug Abuse stamp was not a commemorative but "a warning, a plea for help and a call to the American people to take every step to lift up those who have fallen under the use of drugs, and to strike down those who profit from the misery of others."

Malaria, scourge of much of the world, was conquered by medical research in the 20th century. The symbols on the World United Against Malaria stamp features symbols of the United States and the World Health Organization, a fitting tribute to the worldwide effort to eradicate disease for the common good.

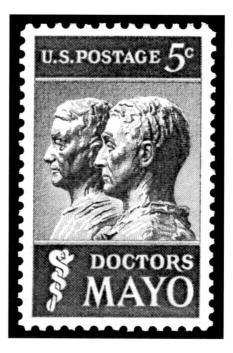

CARE

The letters that make up the acronym CARE originally stood for "Cooperative for American Remittances to Europe," but as the organization expanded its efforts to other parts of the world, CARE now stands for "Cooperative for Assistance and Relief Everywhere." CARE was founded by 22 American humanitarian organizations in 1945 to help provide lifesaving military surplus food to a devastated Europe after the war. This photograph shows CARE packages arriving in Berlin to assist citizens of the beleaguered city. The struggle for control of Berlin was one of the first major confrontations between the Soviet Union and the Allied powers over the fate of Germany after the war. At the end of the war Germany was partitioned into four parts, one each governed by the Soviet Union, the United States, France and England. Berlin was also divided into zones of occupation but the city itself lay deep inside the Soviet zone. On June 24, 1948 the Soviet Union blocked road and rail access to the city and the Allies were faced with supplying the city by air. The Berlin Airlift operated until May 12, 1949, when the Soviet Union reopened the road. The airlift supplied the more than two million civilians and soldiers living in West Berlin with all necessary supplies plus thousands of CARE packages. To honor the relief organization's tremendous contributions in Europe and around the world, this stamp was issued on October 27, 1971.

Peace Corps

The Peace Corps is one of the most visible and enduring symbols of the renaissance of hope in America that marked the early years of the Kennedy Administration. Proposed on the campus of the University of Michigan on October 14, 1960, by John F. Kennedy during his campaign for President, the Peace Corps answered, for thousand of young people of all ages, the question that Kennedy would pose at his inauguration: "Ask what you can do for your country." The Peace Corps was officially established on March 1, 1961. By offering a structure through which Americans can reach out to help those less fortunate than themselves, the Peace Corps changed the lives of some 190,000 volunteers who served in education, health care, agriculture, business and other basic service programs in 74 countries around the world. In this photograph the young man working in a village in Togo is learning as much from the children as they are from him. Returning Peace Corps volunteers frequently comment that the benefits of serving far outweigh the sacrifices made. The average age of a Peace Corps volunteer today is 27, the oldest 80. Most volunteers have an undergraduate degree, 60 percent are female and 93 percent are unmarried. The Peace Corps is still actively recruiting volunteers for service in education, health and the environment. More information can be obtained at www.peacecorps.gov. This stamp was issued on February 11, 1972.

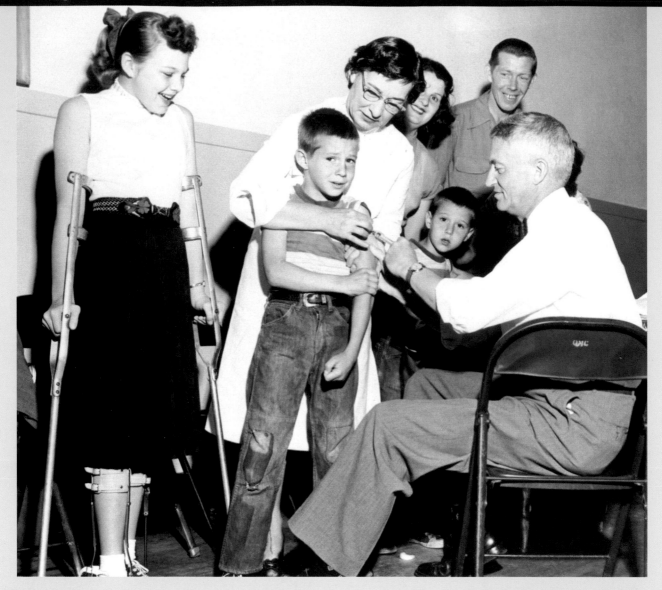

Fighting Polio

Thanks to the efforts of all those who "helped fight polio" the disease is now only a memory in the United States. But in the 1940s and 1950s the United States experienced summer after summer of polio epidemics. Over 100,000 cases of polio occurred between 1952 and 1954 alone. The spread of the disease was poorly understood and families everywhere were terrified that their child might be the next to contract the dread disease. The most famous victim was Franklin D. Roosevelt who contracted polio as an adult and was left paralyzed from the waist down and confined to a wheelchair for the rest of his life. As President, Roosevelt did much to increase awareness of the disease and to encourage those who had contracted it to do everything they could to lead a full life and not let the disease conquer their spirit as well as their bodies. In 1952 Dr. Jonas Salk developed the first polio vaccine. By 1955 a regular program of inoculation was instituted throughout the schools of the nation and millions of children received the vaccine. By 1965 there were only 61 cases of polio reported. In this photograph taken in 1955 Joanne Urnezis, a polio victim, looks on while her six-year-old brother receives the anti-polio vaccine. This stamp was issued on January 15, 1957.

Boy Scouts of America

Founded in England in 1907 by General Robert Baden-Powell, the Boy Scouts is one of the world's successful organizations. It took boys into the outdoors and taught them physical and moral lessons that would serve them for life. Two similar organizations were founded for girls: the Girl Scouts and Camp Fire USA. Thousands of adults volunteered their time to attend meetings, arrange camping trips and give exams so that merit badges could be earned and the boys moved up through the program from Cub Scouts to Boy Scouts to programs for older children. This photograph, taken in 1950, captures the essence of what the movement meant to hundreds of thousands of children and adults – a chance to form a bond, be outdoors and to acknowledge the value of self-sufficiency, hard work, fair play and good fun. The complete Scout Oath, the first words of which appear on this stamp, is: "On my honor I will do my best to do my duty to God and my country and to obey the Scout Law; To help other people at all times; To keep myself physically strong, mentally awake, and

morally straight." The Scout Law states: "A Scout is: Trustworthy, Obedient, Loyal, Cheerful, Helpful, Thrifty, Friendly, Brave, Courteous, Clean, Kind and Reverent." Millions of men today share the bond of being former Scouts. This stamp was issued June 30, 1950.

I do not look upon these United States
as a finished product. We are still
in the making.

– Franklin D. Roosevelt

PART 7

THESE UNITED STATES

THESE UNITED STATES

One of the most fascinating aspects of American history is the way the nation was able – politically and geographically – to expand from 13 colonies into 50 states, reaching first across the continent, then across the Pacific Ocean to Hawaii and across Canada to Alaska. This achievement was not only about conquering distance; it was also about the willingness of generations of Americans to extend the privileges of full citizenship to others. The act passed by Congress to admit new states to the Union clearly specifies that each new state would enter the Union "on an equal footing with the original States in all respects whatever."

Looking back, it could not have been at all obvious to the Founding Fathers at the end of the American Revolution that the original colonies would willingly surrender lands they claimed west of the Allegheny Mountains to the Federal Government. Nor was it certain that they would encourage and support the acquisition of huge tracts of new land west of the Mississippi, or willingly admit other states to full equality with themselves, when doing any of these things would surely diminish their own power and influence in the Federal Government and reduce many smaller states to the status of marginal players on the national scene. Yet that is exactly what happened.

No sooner had the original colonies achieved independence than they set about dealing with the new lands west of the Allegheny Mountains. During the French and Indian War, they had been under the control of France and were the scene of many battles between the British and Colonial forces and the French and their Indian allies. With the defeat of the French and the peace of 1763, control of these lands passed to the British and the colonists were eager to benefit from the victory and expand westward. The British, fearful of the colonies expanding too quickly and concerned with honoring the many treaties they had made with Indian tribes farther west, refused to allow the colonists to settle beyond "the Heads or Sources of any of the Rivers which fall into the Atlantic Ocean from the West and North West." This effectively confined settlement to lands east of the Appalachian Mountains and left the western lands to the Indians "as their Hunting Grounds."

At the end of the Revolutionary War, the victory finally gave the Americans full control over the lands as far west as the Mississippi, and from Lake Superior in the north to the northern boundary of Florida in the south. But this land was not free and clear – virtually all of it was claimed by one or more Indian nations as well as one or more of the 13 original colonies, whose 17th century charters were very vague on boundaries. The question of the future ownership of these lands was an important item of discussion during the first Constitutional Convention and delayed ratification of the Articles of Confederation.

At issue, in this pre-industrial age when ownership of land was still the basis of wealth, was the ability of any state with large land holdings in the west to sell that land to pay its debts and achieve growth without taxing its citizens. If the states with large western land claims were allowed to keep and sell the land, the states without any western land claims and thus without any lands to sell (New Hampshire, Rhode Island, New Jersey, Pennsylvania, Delaware and Maryland) would be at a serious disadvantage.

The Articles of Confederation required the assent of all 13 colonies before they could go into effect. Maryland refused to sign until the issue of western land claims was settled. It proposed that all the colonies cede their western lands to the Federal Government, to be sold and settled for the benefit of all the colonies. Amazingly, all the states with land claims – including Virginia, which laid claim through its original charter to virtually all the land west of the mountains – agreed to this suggestion, thereby putting the good of the nation ahead of the interests of the individual states. The Articles were signed and settlement proceeded; soon the Indians' hunting grounds were no more.

Congress began admitting new states almost immediately; Vermont was admitted in 1791 as the 14th state, Kentucky followed in 1792, Tennessee in 1796 and Ohio in 1802. In the coming 200 years, Congress would admit 33 more states. One, Texas, had been an independent country; some, like Alaska, were the results of specific purchases of land. Most were carved out of the Northwest Territory, the Louisiana Purchase or the lands acquired at the end of the Mexican-American War. Each one of the states has been honored at least once on a postage stamp, usually on the occasion of a significant anniversary of its date of admission into the Union.

DELAWARE: Admitted to the Union on December 7, 1787, as the first state.

Dutch, Swedish and English settlers all arrived in the region in the years after Henry Hudson sailed into Delaware Bay in 1609. Named for Lord De la Warr, who was governor of Virginia at the time, the state came under English control in 1674 and was made a separate colony in 1704. Although initially a reluctant participant in the Revolutionary War, Delaware was the first state to ratify the new U.S. Constitution. Delaware covers 2,489 square miles and has a population of approximately 817,000.

PENNSYLVANIA: Admitted to the Union on December 2, 1787, as the second state. Pennsylvania was originally a grant of land given to William Penn by King Charles II of England in 1682. Penn, a Quaker, believed in peace and religious freedom. He initially brought 360 settlers to the colony, and his good relations with the natives and the colony's spirit of freedom and tolerance soon attracted other settlers. Philadelphia was the center of colonial government for most of the period from 1775 to 1800, when the nation's capital moved to Washington, D.C. Pennsylvania covers 46,055 square miles and has a population of approximately 12,366,000.

NEW JERSEY: Admitted to the Union on December 18, 1787, as the third state.

The Dutch West India Company established a trading post in what is now Trenton as early as 1618 when this land was part of New Netherland. In 1664 the territory was surrendered to the British and renamed New Jersey after the Isle of Jersey in the English Channel. New Jersey became a separate royal colony in 1738 and was later one of the original 13 colonies. New Jersey covers 7,417 square miles and has a population of approximately 8,638,000.

GEORGIA: Admitted to the Union on January 2, 1778, as the fourth state.

Georgia, the last of the 13 original colonies to be established, was named for King George II of England. Hernando de Soto had explored the coast for Spain in 1540, but the English later claimed the land and James Oglethorpe established the first settlement there in 1733. The colony was originally designated as a place for English debtors who had served time in prison, but few were actually sent, as Georgia's plantation economy developed quickly. Georgia joined the Confederacy and was devastated in the last year of the Civil War. Georgia covers 59,906 square miles and has a population of approximately 8,685,000.

CONNECTICUT: Admitted to the Union on January 9, 1788, as the fifth state.

The early Dutch explorer Adriaen Block was the first European to visit what became Connecticut, in 1614. The first English settlers came from Massachusetts Bay Colony with Puritan Thomas Hooker, who with his followers established Connecticut Colony in 1639. They agreed to be bound by the "Fundamental Orders," principles of government set down to secure the good of the colony. Connecticut, for that reason nicknamed the Constitution State, covers 5,543 square miles and has a population of approximately 3,484,000.

MASSACHUSETTS: Admitted to the Union on February 6, 1788, as the sixth state.

The Pilgrims and the Puritans, early English settlers seeking religious freedom, arrived in Massachusetts Bay starting in 1620. In a few years, the community had established a thriving colony that later became the center of resistance to British taxation and ultimately to British rule. The "Boston Tea Party" and many of the early actions of protest that led to the American Revolutionary War took place here. Massachusetts covers 7,840 square miles and has a population of approximately 6,433,000.

MARYLAND: Joined the Union on April 28, 1788, as the seventh state.

In 1632 King Charles I of England granted a royal charter to Lord Baltimore, giving him the northern part of the Virginia Colony, an area that is now the state of Maryland. Many of the early settlers were Roman Catholics, and the Toleration Act passed in the Maryland assembly in 1649 granted freedom of religion to all Christians. At the end of the Revolutionary War, Maryland seceded the lands on which Washington, D.C., is located to the Federal Government. Maryland covers an area of 12,407 square miles and has a population of approximately 5,509,000.

SOUTH CAROLINA: Joined the Union on May 23, 1788, as the eighth state.

The Spanish and French attempted to establish a colony in South Carolina in the 1500s, but the English made the first successful European settlement in 1670. South Carolina was separated from North Carolina and became a royal colony in 1729. Fearing that its plantation economy and way of life would collapse if slavery were ended, South Carolina led a movement to secede from the Union, and the Civil War began here with the attack on Fort Sumter in Charleston Harbor. South Carolina covers an area of 32,020 square miles and has a population of approximately 4,147,000.

NEW HAMPSHIRE: Joined the Union on June 21, 1788, as the ninth state. The first English settlers arrived in 1623 and established fishing villages. New Hampshire, originally a part of Massachusetts, was made a separate royal colony in 1679. The colonists' love of liberty was so strong they issued their own declaration of freedom from England in January 1776, six months before the signing of the Declaration of Independence. New Hampshire covers an area of 9,350 square miles and has a population of approximately 1,288,000.

VIRGINIA: Joined the Union on June 25, 1788, as the 10th state.

The first successful English settlement in North America was established in 1607 at Jamestown, and Virginia became the first royal colony in 1624. The state became one of the richest and most important in the young country. Eight presidents have come from Virginia, including George Washington. Virginia was the scene of major battles and the final acts of surrender in both the Revolutionary War and the Civil War. Virginia covers an area of 42,774 square miles and has a population of approximately 7,368,000.

NEW YORK: Joined the Union on July 26, 1788, as the 11th state.

Although French sailors first explored New York's coastline in 1524, New York was claimed for the Dutch in 1609 and New Amsterdam was founded on Manhattan Island in 1624. The colony came under English control in 1664. New York City has been the most populous city in the country since the first American census was taken in 1790, and the city and state have welcomed millions of immigrants and been a center of trade and commerce since colonial times. New York covers an area of 47,214 square miles and has a population of approximately 19,190,000 people.

NORTH CAROLINA: Joined the Union on November 21, 1789, as the 12th state.

North Carolina traces its history back to Sir Walter Raleigh's ill-fated attempt to found a colony on Roanoke Island in 1587. Although the settlers vanished with no trace, the colony had the distinction of being the birthplace of Virginia Dare, the first English child born in America. In 1653 the English succeeded in establishing the first permanent settlement here, and North Carolina soon developed a prosperous economy based on supplying the Royal Navy with pitch, tar and turpentine. North Carolina covers an area of 53,819 square miles and has a population of approximately 8,407,000.

RHODE ISLAND: Joined the Union on May 29, 1790, as the 13th state.
Roger Williams and his followers left Puritan Massachusetts to find religious freedom, and were the first to settle in Rhode Island. After the Revolution, the state insisted that freedom of worship be written into the Constitution. Only when the Bill of Rights was added and a provision that each state would have two senators in Congress plus representatives based on population did this colony agree to join the Union, the last of the original 13 colonies to do so. The smallest state in the Union, Rhode Island covers an area of only 1,545 square miles and has a population of approximately 1,076,000.

VERMONT: Joined the Union on March 4, 1791 as the 14th state.
Samuel de Champlain first explored what he named "Verts Monts" (green mountains) in 1609, and claimed the land for France. The first French settlement was established in 1666. English settlers began arriving in 1724 and England gained control of the lands in 1763. Vermont declared itself completely independent – even from the other American colonies – in 1777 and issued its own money. The state has the distinction of being the first new state to join the Union after the original 13 colonies. Vermont covers an area of 9,614 square miles and has a population of approximately 619,000.

KENTUCKY: Joined the Union on June 1, 1792 as the 15th state.
Originally a part of Virginia, Kentucky was the first area west of the Appalachian Mountains to be settled by English colonists. James Harrod formed the first permanent settlement in 1774. Daniel Boone opened the Wilderness Road through the Cumberland Gap on the eve of the American Revolution in 1775 and founded Boonesborough. Kentucky, a slave state, remained in the Union during the Civil War, although many of its soldiers fought for the Confederacy. Kentucky covers an area of 39,728 square miles and has a population of approximately 4,118,000.

TENNESSEE: Joined the Union on June 1, 1796, as the 16th state.

Originally explored by Hernando de Soto and claimed for Spain, Tennessee was later explored and claimed by both England and France. The English acquired control with the Treaty of Paris in 1763, and permanent settlement soon began. Tennessee was the first state to be formed from a government territory. The last state to join the Confederacy, Tennessee was also the first to be readmitted to the Union at the end of the Civil War. Tennessee covers an area of 42,143 square miles and has a population of approximately 5,842,000.

OHIO: Joined the Union on March 1, 1803, as the 17th state.

The Ohio River Valley's rich and abundant farmland made the territory a major prize in the battle between the French and English. First explored by the French, it was the scene of many battles during the French and Indian War before control passed to the English with the Treaty of Paris treaty in 1763. The completion of the Erie Canal in 1825 opened the Northwest to settlement and provided a way for Ohio to ship its produce to eastern markets. Ohio covers an area of 44,825 square miles and has a population of approximately 11,436,000.

LOUISIANA: Joined the Union on April 30, 1812, as the 18th state. Spanish explorers visited this region as early as 1519, but French explorers claimed it in 1682. The French named the entire Mississippi watershed "Louisiana" in honor of King Louis XIV. Situated at the mouth of the Mississippi River, Louisiana controls access to the main natural highway into the center of the nation. It became a French crown colony in 1731 but was given to Spain at the Treaty of Paris in 1763. After being returned to France in 1800, it was sold to the United States in 1803 as the most important part of the Louisiana Purchase. Louisiana covers an area of 43,562 square miles and has a population of approximately 4,496,000.

INDIANA: Joined the Union on December 11, 1816, as the 19th state.

Indiana, "Land of the Indians," sits squarely in the middle of what was the Northwest Territory. It was part of French North America until the Treaty of Paris in 1763. George Rogers Clark commanded the American forces here during the Revolutionary War, and Indiana was the site of the Battle of Fallen Timbers in 1794, which ended the warfare between the Indians and the American settlers. Indiana covers an area of 36,418 square miles and has a population of approximately 6,196,000 people.

MISSISSIPPI: Joined the Union on December 10, 1817, as the 20th state.

In 1540 the Spanish explorer Hernando de Soto was the first European to visit Mississippi, but the French claimed the region in 1699. Great Britain acquired the area in 1763 and surrendered its claim to the United States at the end of the Revolutionary War. Spain, however, did not give up its claim and the land along the coast remained a disputed area until 1810, when the United States formally annexed the territory of West Florida and established the present state boundary. Mississippi covers an area of 48,430 square miles and has a population of approximately 2,881,000.

ILLINOIS: Joined the Union on December 3, 1818, as the 21st state.

Illinois was first visited by Jacques Marquette and Louis Joliet in 1673, and French explorers established the first permanent settlement in 1699. The territory passed to the British in 1763 and then to the United States. The Erie Canal brought settlers west, and the state's position at the south end of Lake Michigan with a connection to the Mississippi via the Illinois River made Chicago a hub of traffic and communication across the country. Illinois covers an area of 55,584 square miles and has a population of approximately 12,654,000.

ALABAMA: Admitted to the Union on December 17, 1819, as the 22nd state.

Spanish explorers visited the area as early as 1519, but the first permanent European settlement was made by the French in 1702. After the Treaty of Paris in 1763 the English assumed control of the area until the American Revolution. Alabama Territory was formed in 1817, two years before the state was admitted to the Union. The Confederacy was founded in Montgomery in 1861 when the state's economy was primarily agricultural, based on large cotton plantations. Alabama covers 52,419 square miles and has a population of approximately 4,500,000.

MAINE: Joined the Union on March 15, 1820, as the 23rd state. After early exploration by both the French and English, permanent English settlement in Maine was established in the 1620s. The territory of Maine was at first part of Massachusetts, but it gained independence and statehood in 1820 when it was admitted to the Union as a "free state" along with Missouri, a "slave state," in the famous Missouri Compromise designed to preserve the balance of free and slave states in Congress. Maine covers an area of 30,862 square miles and has a population of approximately 1,306,000.

MISSOURI: Joined the Union on August 10, 1821, as the 24th state. Despite entering the Union as a slave state and although thousands of its citizens fought for the South, Missouri did not join the Confederacy. Missouri is the meeting place of two of America's greatest rivers – the Mississippi and the Missouri – which meet at St. Louis, making it the largest and most important inland port in the country. Missouri was also the starting point of the Oregon Trail and the Santa Fe Trail, which led thousands of settlers west to the frontier from Independence, Missouri. Missouri covers an area of 69,704 square miles and has a population of approximately 5,704,000.

ARKANSAS: Joined the Union on June 15, 1836, as the 25th state. Hernando de Soto was the first European to reach the state and took possession for Spain in 1541. French explorers arrived in the 1670s, and Henri de Tonti founded the first permanent European settlement on the Arkansas River in 1686. Arkansas became part of the United States in 1803 on land bought from Napoleon's France as part of the Louisiana Purchase, and Arkansas Territory was formed in 1819. The state joined the Confederacy during the Civil War. Arkansas covers an area of 53,179 square miles and has a population of approximately 2,726,000.

MICHIGAN: Joined the Union on January 26, 1837, as the 26th state. French voyageurs were the first Europeans to explore Michigan, establishing settlements at Sault Ste. Marie in 1668 and at Detroit in 1701. The area passed to the British at the end of the French and Indian War with the Treaty of Paris of 1763, and then to the United States at the end of the American Revolution. Michigan Territory was formed in 1805. With the opening of the Erie Canal in 1825, the territory soon acquired a large enough population to qualify for statehood. Michigan covers an area of 96,716 square miles and has a population of approximately 10,080,000.

FLORIDA: Joined the Union on March 3, 1845, as the 27th state.

The Spanish were the first Europeans to reach Florida. Seeking the fabled "fountain of youth," Ponce de Leon visited the area in 1519. St. Augustine, the oldest city in the United States, was founded in 1565. Spain lost Florida to the British in 1763 at the end of the French and Indian War but regained possession in 1783. The United States finally acquired the territory from Spain in 1819 and took possession in 1821. The state joined the Confederacy during the Civil War. Florida covers an area of 53,927 square miles and has a population of approximately 17,019,000.

TEXAS: Joined the Union on December 29, 1845, as the 28th state. Texas has a unique place in American history. It is the only state to have once been an independent country. The Spanish were the first Europeans to reach Texas, arriving on the Gulf Coast in 1519. The area remained a Spanish possession until 1836, when American settlers defeated Mexican General Antonio Lopez de Santa Anna and declared their independence. The short-lived Republic of Texas was annexed as a state in 1845, when its present boundaries were established. Texas joined the Confederacy during the Civil War. Texas covers an area of 268,581 square miles and has a population of approximately 22,119,000.

IOWA: Joined the Union on December 28, 1846, as the 29th state.

French explorers Marquette and Joliet came down the Mississippi into Iowa in 1673 and claimed the Mississippi watershed for France. The United States obtained possession as part of the Louisiana Purchase from Napoleon in 1803. When the first farmers arrived on the prairie, the topsoil in places was as much as five feet deep, and agriculture thrived. Iowa became a territory in 1838. Iowa covers an area of 56,272 square miles and has a population of approximately 2,944,000.

WISCONSIN: Joined the Union on May 29, 1848, as the 30th state. French explorer Jean Nicolet reached Wisconsin in 1634, and the area remained part of the French American empire until the Treaty of Paris in 1763. It then passed to the British, who established the first permanent European settlement at Green Bay in 1764. The United States acquired control of the lands at the end of the Revolutionary War, but British troops remained in the territory until the War of 1812. Wisconsin Territory was formed in 1836. Wisconsin covers an area of 65,498 square miles and has a population of approximately 5,472,000.

CALIFORNIA: Joined the Union on September 9, 1850, as the 31st state. Juan Rodriguez Cabrillo claimed California for Spain in 1542 but regular colonization did not begin until 1769 when the mission at San Diego was established. In 1847, during the Mexican-American War, control passed to the United States. A year later gold was discovered at Sutter's Mill and thousands of Americans rushed to the state to seek their fortune. By 1850, when it became a state, it already had a population of about 100,000 people. California covers an area of 163,696 square miles and has a population of approximately 35,484,000.

MINNESOTA: Joined the Union on May 11, 1858, as the 32nd state. French explorers reached Minnesota on their journey south along Lake Michigan and claimed the area for France in 1679. Part of the land that was to become Minnesota was acquired from the British after the Revolutionary War, and the western parts were acquired from France with the Louisiana Purchase in 1803. The northern boundary with Canada was established in 1818. By 1820 the United States army had established Fort Snelling, and the territory was opened for settlement in the 1850s. Minnesota covers an area of 86,939 square miles and has a population of approximately 5,059,000.

OREGON: Joined the Union on February 14, 1859 as the 33rd state. Spanish and English sailors probably sighted the coast of Oregon in the 1600s but it was not until 1792 that Robert Gray, sailing in the *Columbia*, claimed the territory for the United States. Meriwether Lewis and William Clark, leading the first American overland expedition to the Pacific, explored the area in 1805. The northern boundary of Oregon Territory was not resolved until 1846 when the border between Canada and the United States was established. Oregon covers an area of 98,381 square miles and has a population of approximately 3,560,000.

KANSAS: Joined the union on January 29, 1861, as the 34th state.
The Spanish were the first Europeans to reach Kansas when Francisco de Coronado came north to the Great Plains in 1541. Sieur de la Salle claimed the area for France in 1682, and it came under the control of the United States in 1803 as part of the Louisiana Purchase. Kansas was the site of violence over the extension of slavery into the territories before the Civil War. The state joined the Union as a free state on the eve of the war. Kansas covers an area of 82,277 square miles and has a population of approximately 2,724,000.

WEST VIRGINIA: Joined the Union on June 20, 1863, as the 35th state.
The lands that now comprise West Virginia were first part of the British Virginia Colony from 1607 to 1776, and then part of the state of Virginia. The first permanent settlement in the state was established in 1727. Isolated by the mountains from the slavery-dependent plantation economy of the rest of the state, West Virginia refused to join the Confederacy and decided to break away from Virginia and remain loyal to the Union. It was admitted to the Union in 1863. West Virginia covers an area of 24,230 square miles and has a population of approximately 1,810,000.

NEVADA: Joined the Union on October 31, 1864, as the 36th state. The Spanish crossed the state on their way to California but no permanent settlements were established. The area became part of the United States at the end of the Mexican-American War in 1848 and the first permanent settlement began in 1851. The discovery of rich deposits of silver and gold in the famous Comstock Lode in 1859 brought thousands of miners into the area and the Territory of Nevada was established in 1861. Nevada receives only about 7 inches of rain a year, less than any other state. Nevada covers an area of 110,561 square miles and has a population of approximately 2,241,000.

NEBRASKA: Joined the Union on March 1, 1867, as the 37th state. Part of Nebraska was acquired with the Louisiana Purchase from France in 1803 and part from the lands acquired after the Mexican-American War in 1848. Lewis and Clark explored the area, and the first settlement was established in 1823. Settlers arrived in larger numbers in the 1860s with the completion of the transcontinental railroad. Nebraska covers an area of 77,872 square miles and has a population of 1,739,000.

COLORADO: Joined the Union on August 1, 1876, as the 38th state.
In 1706 Juan de Ulibarri claimed the land that became Colorado for Spain. When gold was discovered in 1858 north of Pike's Peak, thousands of fortune seekers rushed into the area and Colorado Territory was formed in 1861. With the arrival of the railroad in 1870, Colorado was linked to the rest of the nation. With an average elevation of 6,800 feet above sea level, Colorado has the highest elevation of any state in the nation. Colorado covers an area of 104,094 square miles and has a population of approximately 4,551,000.

NORTH DAKOTA: Joined the Union on November 2, 1889, as the 39th state.
SOUTH DAKOTA: Joined the Union on November 2, 1889, as the 40th state.

The vast Dakota Territory was first explored by French-Canadian fur traders in 1738. In 1803 most of it was acquired by the United States through the Louisiana Purchase. The first permanent settlement was established in 1817 at Fort Pierre in South Dakota. Dakota Territory, containing what are now North and South Dakota, was formed in 1861 but the remote location and land disputes with the Indians delayed settlement. The territory was divided and North and South Dakota were admitted to the Union on the same day in 1889. North Dakota covers an area of 70,700 square miles and has a population of approximately 633,000. South Dakota covers an area of 77,117 square miles and has a population of approximately 764,000.

MONTANA: Joined the Union on November 8, 1889, as the 41st state. Lewis and Clark traveled extensively through the area after the Louisiana Purchase in 1803. The western portion of the state was acquired by the United States when the Oregon Treaty with Great Britain settled the location of the border between Canada and the United States. Cattle, wheat and lumber sustained early settlers, but it was the discovery of gold and massive copper deposits that drew speculators and miners to the state in the 1860s. Montana Territory was organized in 1864. Montana covers an area of 145,552 square miles and has a population of approximately 918,000.

WASHINGTON: Joined the Union on November 11, 1889, as the 42nd state.

Spanish, British, Russian and American sailors visited the Pacific coast of Washington in the late 1700s. Lewis and Clark's expedition explored the Columbia River region and claimed the land for the United States in 1805. After a period of territorial dispute with England, the Treaty of Oregon established the border between the United States and Canada in 1846. Washington Territory was carved out from the vast Oregon Territory in 1853. Washington covers an area of 71,300 square miles and has a population of approximately 6,131,000.

IDAHO: Joined the Union on July 3, 1890, as the 43rd state.

Lewis and Clark crossed southern Utah in 1805 and were quickly followed by trappers eager for the beaver pelts in great demand in the east. By the 1860s miners had found gold, silver, and other minerals and gems, and Idaho's mining boom had begun. Idaho Territory was formed in 1863 and its population was already 90,000 when it was admitted to the Union in 1890. Idaho covers an area of 83,570 square miles and has a population of approximately 1,366,000.

WYOMING: Joined the Union on July 10, 1890, as the 44th state.

The most likely first European visitors to Wyoming were French trappers and members of the Lewis and Clark expedition in 1807. Wyoming Territory was formed in 1868 and its nickname, "Equality State," comes from the fact that in 1869, 21 years before it joined the Union, it granted women the right to vote. The state has an average elevation of more than a mile and is the least populated state in the Union. Wyoming covers an area of 97,814 square miles and has a population of approximately 501,000.

UTAH: Joined the Union on January 4, 1896, as the 45th state. The first Europeans to explore Utah were Spanish Franciscan missionaries who arrived in 1776. Brigham Young and his band of Mormon followers traveled across the west seeking a place remote enough for them to practice their religion in peace. In 1847 they arrived at a great salt lake – its water is more than four times as salty as the ocean – and founded the first settlement. Utah Territory was organized in 1850 and by 1860 it had a population of over 40,000 Mormons. Utah covers an area of 84,899 square miles and has a population of approximately 2,351,000.

OKLAHOMA: Joined the Union on November 16, 1907, as the 46th state.

Francisco Vasquez de Coronado was the first European to explore the area, in 1541. The United States acquired the territory as part of the Louisiana Purchase in 1803. Before being opened to settlement, Oklahoma was part of Indian Territory established in 1834 and was home to members of over 60 tribes who had been forced off their lands in other parts of the country. In 1889, on the first day of homesteading, over 50,000 people competed for land. Oklahoma Territory was established the following year. Oklahoma covers an area of 68,667 square miles and has a population of approximately 3,512,000.

NEW MEXICO: Joined the Union on January 6, 1912, as the 47th state.

Although Vasquez de Coronado had explored the region as early as 1540, it was not until 1598 that the Spanish established the first permanent European settlement on the Rio Grande River. Santa Fe was founded in 1610 and became the capital of the Spanish region of New Mexico. The United States took control after the Mexican-American War and the southern border with Mexico was established with the Gadsden Purchase in 1853. New Mexico covers 121,590 square miles and has a population of approximately 1,875,000.

ARIZONA: Joined the Union on February 14, 1912, as the 48th state. Spanish Franciscan priests who accompanied and followed the earliest explorers established most of the early settlements in the Arizona region. The Spanish mission San Xavier del Bac was begun in 1692 but it was not until 1775 that the Spanish established Fort Tucson. After the Mexican-American War the United States took control of the territory, and Arizona became the last of the continental states to join the Union early in the last century. Arizona covers 113,998 square miles and has a population of approximately 5,581,000.

ALASKA: Joined the Union on January 3, 1959, as the 49th state.

The Alaskan mainland was not explored by Europeans until 1741 when Vitus Bering, a Danish explorer employed by Russia, visited the area and claimed it for Russia. Alaska remained largely unexplored except along the coast, and Secretary of State William Steward negotiated its purchase from Russia in 1867 for $7,200,000, about two cents an acre. In 1880 the first census recorded only 430 non-native settlers in the state but the discovery of gold in 1898 attracted more than 30,000 to the state. More than twice as large as Texas, it makes up one-sixth of the area of the United States. Alaska covers 663,267 square miles and has a population of approximately 649,000.

HAWAII: Joined the Union on August 21, 1959, as the 50th state. Polynesians who arrived from other Pacific islands were the first to settle the eight main islands that make up Hawaii. In 1778 Captain James Cook claimed them for Britain and named them the Sandwich Islands in honor of the Earl of Sandwich. Hawaii remained an independent sovereign state until a revolution in 1893 ended the monarchy. In 1900 the islands were annexed by the United States and became a territory. Hawaii covers an area of 10,931 square miles and has a population of 1,257,000

WASHINGTON, DISTRICT OF COLUMBIA: Established in 1790. The nation's capital was placed midway between the northern and southern colonies. In 1790 Maryland donated land for the capital district along the Potomac River, and George Washington made the final selection of the location of the capital buildings. The capital was officially moved from Philadelphia to Washington on December 1, 1800. The District of Columbia (named for Columbus) is not a state but has a municipal government under the jurisdiction of Congress. Washington, D.C., covers an area of 68 square miles and has a population of approximately 563,000.

PART 8

THE
ART
OF THE
STAMP

THE ART OF THE STAMP

by Terrence W. McCaffrey

It's often been said that the only constant is change, but that's not true when it comes to the United States postage stamp program. Certainly there have been some very important changes in the program but the three most important did not occur until more than 1,000 stamps had been issued, over a century after the first American postage stamp had appeared in 1847.

For the first 110 years, give or take a year or two, the Post Office gave us beautifully engraved, single-color stamps that rank right up there with the best of their kind produced anywhere in the world. Technological changes allowed the inclusion of a second color occasionally, but rarely. It wasn't until the late 1950s that the first full-color stamps were produced. But the big changes in the program, the pivotal decisions that occurred in the years 1957, 1973 and 1994, were more about policy and design than printing technology.

The first big change in the United States stamp program happened in 1957 with the formation of the Citizens' Stamp Advisory Committee. Until then, stamps honoring specific industries, associations and anniversaries dominated the annual program, and members of Congress were in the habit of recommending the subjects to be honored on these stamps. In the 1930s and 1940s not only Congress but also Franklin D. Roosevelt, the President of the United States and himself an avid stamp collector, was deeply involved in the process of stamp design and subject selection. Numerous articles have been written about FDR's love of stamp collecting. His passion for stamps led him not only to suggest stamp subjects but also to actually design stamps!

Many of the stamps issued during FDR's four terms in office were developed from a quick sketch made by Mr. Roosevelt and whisked over to the Post Office Department. His final act as president, just before his death, was to sketch out a design for the "Toward United Nations" stamp, a fitting tribute to his hope for world peace at the end of the war. Worthy as the subject was, this stamp joined dozens of others honoring specific industries and associations that were favorites of the nation's leaders, for personal or political reasons.

The proverbial straw that broke the camel's back, or as it might be said in this case, "the chicken that laid the egg," was the 1948 Poultry Industry Centennial stamp. The American public wanted to know, "What is a chicken doing on a postage stamp? And furthermore, why would I want to buy it?" After several years of indecision in the late 1940s and early 1950s on how to respond to the public outcry about the subjects being honored on our stamps, the Post Office Department felt it was time to take control of the program and provide stamps the American public actually wanted to buy and use. In 1957 the Post Office Department, under Postmaster General Arthur Summerfield, formed the Citizens' Stamp Advisory Committee (CSAC). The seven-member committee was charged with providing guidance on the selection of stamp subjects and assisting in design development. Up to that time, the Bureau of Engraving and Printing (BEP) had provided stamp design, as it had done since the turn of the twentieth century.

Members of the Advisory Committee were selected from the professional ranks of the business, academic and design worlds. They got off to a slow start, meeting only a few times in the first year or so, but they soon found their footing, and over the next 50 years selected and approved designs for thousands of stamps. It's often pointed out that in the first 100 years after 1847 the United States issued fewer than 1,000 stamps, but that over 2,000 stamps were issued between 1951 and 2007. This major increase is due in part to the population explosion, the growth of stamp collecting as a hobby and the public's insatiable appetite for something new and different. Since 1957 the CSAC has guided the stamp program's growth in size and scope.

In the early 1960s, when the CSAC began its work, the Post Office was still only issuing an average of 15 to 20 stamps annually and the subject selection process was relatively easy. The American public were not aware they could recommend stamp subjects to the Post Office. That has changed. Today the Office of Stamp Development receives more than 50,000 letters a year about the stamp program. Many letters give feedback, both pro and con, on the stamps just issued, but many contain recommendations for stamp subjects such as famous scientists, celebrities, authors and other prominent individuals. People often ask to have one of their relatives honored for what they feel was a major contribution to our society. But we've also received letters recommending such whimsical subjects as the American Hamburger, the Hot Dog, Hate (to counter our Love stamp series) and even a nostalgic "Passing of the American Outhouse" stamp, complete with a design featuring the quarter moon in the door!

To guide the Post Office through this maze of suggestions and special interests, the CSAC approximately 40 years ago established a set of criteria for selecting stamp subjects. The criteria have changed little over the years, the most notable point being what we internally call the "sufficiently dead" rule. For many years the rule was that a person had to be deceased for 10 years before they could be commemorated on a stamp. In 2007 this was changed to five years, to make the program more contemporary and relevant.

Many stamp purists still insist that we violate this rule every time we depict a living person on a stamp. What they don't realize is that the rule prevents an individual from being commemorated on a stamp for five years, but it doesn't prevent the use of a living person's image on a stamp. If a living person is used as a model, as on the 1997 Ballet stamp where we used a photograph of a ballerina to celebrate the art of ballet, the image is acceptable under our rules even though the model herself was certainly not dead. But certain factions within the collecting community still take issue with it. There are two other important criteria: no stamps can be issued to honor organizations or associations – without this rule we would be inundated with requests from thousands of organizations nationwide; and anniversaries can be commemorated in 50-year increments only, to avoid 10, 20, 25 – or even 35-year – anniversary requests, which we receive by the thousands anyway.

Over the years the Citizens' Stamp Advisory Committee has grown from its original seven members to a maximum of 15 today. Members are chosen by the Postmaster General for their expertise in their respective fields. The Postal Service makes every effort to include diversity in race, gender and professional disciplines.

Among the notable committee members over the years have been the internationally famous artist Andrew Wyeth and later, his son Jamie; James A. Michener, the prolific best selling author; movie actors Ernest Borgnine and Karl Malden; Richard "Digger" Phelps, the famed basketball coach and ESPN sports commentator; and the pre-eminent African American children's book author and three-time Caldecott Medal winner, Jerry Pinkney. Numerous other experienced historians, professors, marketing experts, and design professionals, whose dedication and insight have been invaluable, have also offered their expertise.

CSAC meetings are held quarterly for two days to review new stamp subjects and designs. Meetings take place behind closed doors and are considered confidential; deliberations and decisions are more candid and constructive that way. No stamp proponents are allowed to attend the meetings to petition the group. If that were to happen, the committee would have to sit full-time to handle the high number of requests for meetings.

For many years after the CSAC was formed, the Bureau of Engraving and Printing (BEP) continued to be involved not only in printing stamps but also in their design development. As the years passed, the design process was influenced more and more by leading designers and illustrators who either served as committee members or were hired by the committee to act as art directors or, as they were called for many years, "Design Coordinators." In 1959 Stevan Dohanos was selected to work with the committee to oversee a design overhaul of the program. Dohanos was at the time one of the most respected illustrators in the country, having done several covers for *The Saturday Evening Post* in the 1940s and 1950s. In the mid 1960s Dohanos was appointed to the committee, and eventually became its Chair in 1974. One of his accomplishments was to reduce the BEP's influence by commissioning leading illustrators to assist in stamp design, notably Norman Rockwell, who created two stamps, the 1960 "Boy Scouts of America" and the 1963 "City Mail Delivery."

By 1969 a second design coordinator was needed to handle the growing workload. Dohanos brought Bradbury Thompson, the dean of American typographers and one of the most important graphic designers of the day, into the process. The 1960s and 1970s are known as the "Westport period of stamp design." Dohanos and Thompson both lived in this southwestern region of Connecticut, noted for its artists' colony, and many stamps commissioned during these decades were by artists who also lived in this area. With the advent of improved printing technology, the stamp program began to blossom into full color, replete with designs and illustrations by America's leading artists. Thompson's influence, relative to typography alone, was major. In the more than 100 stamps that Thompson designed, he developed a unified look in the way the denomination was treated. For example, United States Postage 20 cents was reduced to a glyphic USA20c. This simplification gave stamp designers additional freedom and space to develop better, cleaner designs. Dohanos and Thompson retained some degree of involvement with the stamp program until 1989 and 1992, respectively. Their contributions to the program made a substantial change in the look of United States stamps.

Around 1980 the design coordinators, who had been sitting members of the CSAC, became independent contractors working with postal officials and the committee. This change separated responsibility for stamp creation from the processes of subject choice and design approval. New design coordinators were appointed in the 1980s and 1990s, each selected for his or her prior experience and area of expertise. In the mid-1990s, to more accurately reflect their activities, their title was changed from Design Coordinator to Art Director. Currently there are six art directors under contract to the Postal Service.

The second decision that significantly altered the direction of the stamp program came in 1993, when the "King" changed the stamp world forever – the King being, of course, the one and only Elvis Presley. Before 1993 over 2,500 subjects had been commemorated on United States postage stamps. But none would be as attention getting or make a bigger difference to the program than the one issued in honor of the king of rock and roll. To understand how a single stamp honoring a rock and

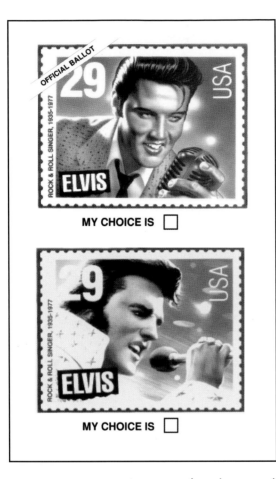

MY CHOICE IS ☐

MY CHOICE IS ☐

roll singer could have such a big impact, we have to look back on the types of stamps issued prior to Elvis.

From the beginning of the stamp program in 1847 until 1893, United States stamps honored only presidents and statesmen. In 1893 the first commemorative stamps, marking the 400th anniversary of Columbus' voyages, changed what we put on our stamps. Over the next 50 years, from about 1900 to 1950, we honored presidents, statesmen and other distinguished individuals as well as all those organizations and associations Congress was so fond of. The Post Office, and as it became in 1972, the United States Postal Service, had begun to include subjects of more general interest, but one area it didn't feel comfortable with was pop culture. Pop culture was always felt to be too frivolous a subject to be worthy of the dignity of a postage stamp – stamps being one of the two forms of United States security, the other being the dollar.

Elvis not only broke records with his concert attendance and hit records; he also broke the pop culture barrier on stamps. But he didn't do it alone. He had the help of then Postmaster General, Anthony M. Frank. PMG Frank wanted to develop a series of stamps on American music and he wanted Elvis Presley to be honored on the first stamp issued. The CSAC balked at the idea of Elvis and turned it down because of what was then felt to be his controversial lifestyle. Because the CSAC is an advisory committee whose function is to make recommendations, it is the prerogative of the Postmaster General to overrule the committee. At a year-end dinner held in honor of the committee, PMG Frank thanked the members for all their hard work and told them of his decision to have the committee proceed with the development of a comprehensive music series, with the assistance of musicologists from the Smithsonian Institution. Then he dropped the bombshell. Despite the committee's concerns about arousing controversy, he wanted the first design for the music series to be the stamp honoring Elvis. It was one of the rare times the CSAC was overruled. Needless to say, the committee acquiesced, and thus began a major transformation in the stamp program.

In addition to his influence on American music, Elvis became the king of the stamp world. A record 500 million commemorative stamps were printed and it was a sellout, generating a record $26 million in stamp retention revenue for the Postal Service. The Elvis stamp still reigns as the king; no other has surpassed it in popularity or retention. The Elvis stamp set a new benchmark for the Postal Service and it was unique in being the first stamp to have its design voted on by the American public. In 1962 the public had been asked to submit designs for the 100th anniversary of the Battle of Gettysburg stamp to be issued in 1963. Postal officials learned a hard lesson with that project, being overwhelmed with thousands of designs to sort through. Not wanting to repeat that mistake, the CSAC commissioned eight different artists to provide images of Elvis. Twenty-six pieces of art were reviewed, everything from rough color sketches to finished paintings. The committee selected two works, one depicting Elvis in the 1950s and one in the 1970s. The public was then invited to choose between them. Thus, the vote was between the "young" or the "old" Elvis. Eventually a painting by Mark Stutzman of the younger Elvis won out over an illustration by John Berkey of the older Elvis.

No advertising dollars were needed to promote this campaign. Elvis sold it for us. The Postal Service produced postcard ballots showing the two images, in black and white, for the public to fill out and mail in. Millions of ballots were printed and *People* magazine was asked to reproduce the ballot in one of its weekly issues as well. In the end, over one-and-a-half million ballots were completed and returned. Seventy-five percent of respondents voted for the young Elvis. The program was a huge success despite the unforeseen dilemma of the ballots being taken from post office lobbies by the handful– we eventually discovered that stamp collectors were taking them. When the stamp was issued, the printed stamps were affixed to the ballots and cancelled on the first day of issue, thus creating unique collectables.

Not only is the Elvis stamp the largest-selling commemorative stamp of all time but it paved the way for numerous other pop culture stamps that have also been extremely popular. Among other notable pop culture icons honored on United States stamps are Marilyn Monroe, Bugs Bunny, James Dean, Mickey Mouse, Superman, Lucille Ball, Frankenstein, Dick Tracy, Clyde McPhatter, Kermit the Frog, Charlie Chaplin, Darth Vader and Yoda, among dozens of others.

The formation of the CSAC and the creation of the Elvis stamp had an impact on the visual look of stamps that was easy for the public to perceive. The third important event – the now infamous Bill Pickett stamp – brought internal change to the stamp development process and had a very dramatic and stressful impact on the program.

Because the stamp development process is so complex, it takes anywhere from one-and-a-half to three years to develop a design today. Up until 1994 the process was not quite as complex. Bill Pickett changed all that. It began in 1992 with an innocuous concept to issue four stamps depicting scenes of the Old West. Easy enough. Or so we thought. As the set evolved, the CSAC decided to include famous people from the era. The list grew and grew. In the end a total of 20 subjects were selected for what was to be the first Classic Collection.

After CSAC identified the 20 Legends of the West subjects, I assigned the art direction to Richard Sheaff, one of our six contract art directors. Mark Hess, a prominent illustrator from Katonah, New York, was chosen to illustrate the 20 stamps, itself a very large undertaking in a short time period. Freelance researchers undertook exhaustive visual research to provide a range of images from which Mark could work.

Bill Pickett, one of the subjects, was easier to research than the others because there were photos of this famous cowboy who worked in rodeos and eventually in the film industry. The most reproduced image of Bill showed him standing next to a rail fence in his cowboy attire. The original negative of the photograph described him as "Bill Pickett, Negro Cowboy." This photograph had appeared, with the same caption, in numerous prestigious publications from the Library of Congress, the Smithsonian Institution and Time Life Books, among others.

To obtain permission for the Legends of the West, we hired a genealogical firm to track down any living relatives of these Old West characters. Approximately 35 years ago, the regulations concerning the reproduction of a person's photograph, likeness or name became more complicated. Until then the Post Office Department had generally commemorated famous individuals without any legal agreements because it was felt that "it was an honor to be on a postage stamp." Still true, but not legal anymore. Since the early 1970s, the Postal Service has had to obtain permission from a person's estate to reproduce that person's image on a stamp.

Our genealogical research firm told us that Bill Pickett had no known living relatives. Unfortunately, we believed them and proceeded to produce the stamps. The print production lead time for the average stamp is four to six months – to print, perforate, cut, package and ship the stamps to 37,000 post offices nationwide. The general rule is that the new stamps must be physically in the post office one month prior to the first day of issue, which in this case was scheduled for spring 1994. Postmasters may, in some instances, choose to open the boxes of new stamps before the first day of issue, instead of reordering current stamps. Such was the case with the Legends of the West. Eighty panes of the Bill Pickett stamps were sold to the public before the scheduled date.

Then unexpectedly, in January 1994 our offices were visited by one of the Pickett relatives, who informed us that the image on the stamp wasn't really Bill, it was his brother Ben. It turned out that there were in fact approximately 120 living relatives of Mr. Pickett, many of whom lived in the suburbs of Washington, D.C. The family had been seeking to have this mistake corrected, but to no avail. They insisted that the stamp be recalled and destroyed. We had no choice but to comply with their wishes. Unfortunately, the 80 panes that had already been sold could not be retrieved. As expected, the news of the stamp error, a phenomenon in the stamp-collecting world, made headlines everywhere. Because of this "error," each of the 80 panes was now valued at $2,000. A nice return on investment, considering the face value of the pane was only $5.80.

The decision was made to reissue the stamp with the correct image, but under the pressure of time constraints I decided to have Mark paint over the portrait of the man we now knew to be Ben Pickett. In hindsight, we should have taken the time to create an entirely new painting. Now, because of a rush decision, the original art for one of the most famous stamp errors is lost, buried beneath layers of paint, under the real Bill Pickett. The stamps were rushed into a second printing in an attempt to release them in the same year as originally planned.

While all of this was going on, Congress chose to become involved. We thought that with the creation of the CSAC, Congress was out of the picture, but they raised concerns as to how much it was costing the Postal Service to correct this error and insisted we find a way to retrieve those costs. We decided to hold a lottery to sell 250,000 copies of the original pane containing the "wrong" Bill Pickett to collectors. The money raised would cover our production costs.

With little publicity we received over 425,000 entries in a matter of days. We held the lottery, sent the "incorrect" panes to the lucky 250,000 winners, and thought everything was fine. It was not to be. With the release of the additional quarter-million "incorrect" panes, the collectors who had purchased the original 80 panes, which had been valued at $2,000, now found their pane worth only $200, so they decided to sue the Postal Service. After more than a year of legal wrangling, they lost their case and the current value of the pane is still around $200. The lesson we learned is that you need to be very sure you have permission for anything you reproduce, especially if it's used on a postage stamp. I have found over the years that postage stamps are among the most scrutinized works of art around. Everyone is looking to find an "error" and strike it rich.

This saga of the Bill Pickett stamp is by way of saying that the third pivotal change in the stamp program was due to an Old West cowboy. Because of that misidentified photograph, the Postal Service implemented a very complex system of research, verification and rights clearance, unequaled in the world. We now have an entire firm contracted to provide visual reference, fact verification, rights identification and numerous other details associated with the stamp program. While the process now takes more time than it used to, hopefully it will prevent any future Bill Pickett incidents. It was a hard lesson to learn, but a worthwhile one in the long term.

Over the past 50 years the stamp program has undergone numerous other changes, both large and small, but none as significant as these three. Some stamp collectors may disagree and point to the advent of self-adhesive stamps as a major change. While this is true, it's a production milestone, of which there have been many in the past 50 years. But as far as shaping the look and direction of the stamp program goes, these have been the major milestones. Who would have thought that a chicken, a rock and a roll singer, and a cowboy would have so great an impact on a national stamp program?

Because of my position at the Postal Service, I'm often asked, "What's your personal favorite stamp?" It's probably the most difficult question for me to answer. I frequently respond, diplomatically, by saying that it's difficult for me to choose one favorite, because for the past 17 years I've nurtured over 1,500 stamps into being, and I consider all of them to be like my children. But, when pressed, there is one stamp that I feel very close to: the Breast Cancer Awareness semi-postal issued in 1998. I like this one not merely because of its important subject matter and the fact that it has raised over $54 million for breast cancer research, but also for its incredibly unique

design. Dozens of concepts were pursued before this beautiful solution to the question of how to graphically deal with this delicate subject was arrived at through the combined talents of Ethel Kessler, the stamp designer, and Whitney Sherman, the illustrator. I'm sure this stamp will continue to resonate with me and with millions of others in the future.

Among the earlier engraved stamps, the 1922 Definitive issue has always been a favorite of mine for a number of reasons. The beautifully designed and engraved border is a wonderful unifying element for the series. The contrasting subject choices – Niagara Falls and the U.S. Capitol building, for example – made the series even more unique. I believe this series was one of the first attempts by the Post Office Department to use American scenes and symbols, such as the bison, on stamps that weren't intended to commemorate a specific event. The latter part of the series, which included the $1.00 Lincoln Memorial, was issued within a year of the memorial's dedication. Designing for definitive stamps is even more difficult than designing commemoratives because of the smaller palette on which to create these miniature masterpieces.

Another common question that I'm frequently asked, again without an easy answer, is: "What is the future of postage stamps in the wake of ever-changing technological advances, such as the computer and e-mail?" Who would have guessed 30 years ago what the computer would do to our society? Who can predict the future of stamps and of letters themselves? Will they go the way of the dinosaur and become a thing of the past? Will there be a future in creating stamps solely as collectibles, and not postage? Only time can answer these questions. But in the interim I hope that you have a greater appreciation of our postage stamps and the wealth of information, knowledge and art that comes with each and every one of these little pieces of paper. Small as it may be, each stamp carries a powerful message, both through the information it imparts and through the works of art captured on such a small scale. The next time you receive a letter, take a good look at the message carried by that colorful little stamp in the upper right corner, and remember the level of loving care that went into its creation. After all, stamps are our nation's calling cards.

Terrence W. McCaffrey
Manager, Stamp Development, Stamp Services
United States Postal Service

CREDITS

ACKNOWLEDGMENTS

Many people besides the authors deserve credit for this book. Barbara Campbell, Managing Editor at Firefly Books, helped bring it to fruition in a myriad of ways. Her unfailing support and patience are greatly appreciated. Lionel Koffler, the President of Firefly Books, not only gave us the idea, but also provided enthusiasm for the book and support for the authors.

The staff at the Smithsonian National Postal Museum in Washington, D.C., was extraordinarily kind and helpful. Cheryl Ganz, who wrote the Introduction to the book, also provided editorial guidance and suggestions that resulted in a better book. James O'Donnell's contribution cannot be overstated. He not only sourced digital images for many of the stamps but also provided encouragement and guidance and opened doors along the way. Throughout the process his patience and cooperation never waned.

At the United States Post Office, in addition to Terrence McCaffrey whose essay on stamp design so nicely closes this book, Courtney Loy provided much help in clearing permissions and endured many requests for information as the list of stamps to be included in the book constantly changed.

Bob Wilcox, a friend as well as the book's designer, provided the design and layout as well as his usual unflappable calm in the face of tight deadlines. Barbara Hicks and the staff at General Printers provided a quiet office in which to work during a critical period in the writing.

Finally, to Karen, Katherine, Allison and Shannon, who put up with the long hours and preoccupation that a work of this length requires, we owe a great debt for their encouragement and support and dedicate this book to them.

FURTHER READING

Axelrod, Alan and Charles Phillips. *What Every American Should Know About American History*. Avon, MA: Adams Media, 2004.

Bailyn, Bernard et al. *The Great Republic*. Boston: Little Brown, 1977.

Bockenhauer, Mark and Stephen Cunha. *Our Fifty States*. Washington, D.C: National Geographic, 2004.

Cooke, Alistair. *Alistair Cooke's America*. London: Weidenfeld & Nicolson, 2002.

Corelison, Pam and Ted Yanak. *The Great American History Fact-Finder*. Boston: Houghton Mifflin, 2004.

Gordon, Lois and Alan Gordon. *American Chronicle, Seven Decades in American Life*. New York: Crown Publishers, 1990.

Johnson, Paul. *A History of the American People*. New York: Harper Collins, 1997.

Juell, Rodney and Steven Rod eds. *Encyclopedia of United States Stamps and Stamp Collecting*. Minneapolis, MN: Kirk House, 2006.

Kennedy, David M. *Freedom from Fear, The American People in Depression and War*. Volume IX of The Oxford History of the United States. New York: Oxford, 1999.

Klug, Janet and Sundman, Donald J. *100 Greatest American Stamps*. Atlanta, GA: Whitman Publishing Company, 2007.

McCullough, David. *John Adams*. New York: Simon & Schuster, 2001.

Miller, James and John Thompson. *Almanac of American History*. Washington, D.C.: National Geographic, 2006.

Nisenson, Samuel & Franklin Gollings. *Great Moments in American History*. New York: Lion Press, 1967.

Schweikart, Larry and Michael Allen. *A Patriot's History of the United States*. New York: Sentinel, 2004.

Smith, Carter. *Presidents, Every Question Answered*. Irving, NY: Hylas Publishing, 2005.

Urdang, Lawrence, ed. *The Timetables of American History*. New York: Simon & Schuster, 1996.

STAMP CATALOGUES

Postal Service Guide to U.S. Stamps, The. 34th Edition. New York: United States Postal Services, 2007.

Scott 2007 Specialized Catalogue of United States Postage Stamps & Covers. Sidney, Ohio: Scott Publishing Co, 2007.

Mystic Stamp Company On Line Catalogue www.mysticstamp.com

WEBSITES

Smithsonian National Postal Museum www.postalmuseum.si.edu/

Publication 100 – The United States Postal Service, An American History 1775 – 2006 www.usps.com/history/history/his1.htm

Mystic Stamp Company www.mysticstamp.com

STAMP INDEX BY PAGE NUMBER

STAMP INDEX BY PAGE NUMBER

STAMP INDEX BY PAGE NUMBER

STAMP INDEX BY PAGE NUMBER

STAMP INDEX BY PAGE NUMBER

STAMP INDEX BY PAGE NUMBER

STAMP INDEX BY NAME

STAMP INDEX BY NAME

STAMP INDEX BY NAME

GENERAL INDEX